STRATFORD
TO
CHESHUNT

Vic Mitchell and Dave Brennand

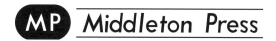
MP Middleton Press

Front Cover: A class 15 British Thompson-Houston Type 1 Bo-Bo 800 H.P. diesel approaches Brimsdown station with a short freight for Temple Mills yard on 29th August 1965. The Lea Valley line was once a hive of industry, goods yards and mixed freight trains with a wide variety of motive power. Sadly, this has all changed and the yards, goods loops and signal boxes have all disappeared. The modern railway lacks the character which can only be immortalised through wonderful old photographs such as this. (D. Fairhurst)

Back Cover Upper: Prior to the electrification of the Lea Valley line in 1969, local stopping services were in the hands of DMUs. Here we see a Derby built class 125 unit on a Liverpool Street bound service arriving at Northumberland Park. These units were introduced in 1958 mainly for the Lea Valley line. (D. Fairhurst)

Back Cover Lower: Viewed shortly after the branch line to Angel Road had been severed, we are looking towards Enfield Town and Bury Street Junction on the 27th June 1965. Edmonton Junction box was reduced to the status of a ground frame controlling the remaining crossover points on the main line after the facing points were removed in 1971. It officially closed in 1979 and was only partially demolished. The lever frame stayed in situ looking rather macabre for a long time after the box itself disappeared. (D. Fairhurst)

Published January 2014

ISBN 978 1 908174 53 6

© Middleton Press, 2014

Design Deborah Esher

Published by
    Middleton Press
    Easebourne Lane
    Midhurst
    West Sussex
    GU29 9AZ
Tel: 01730 813169
Fax: 01730 812601
Email: info@middletonpress.co.uk
www.middletonpress.co.uk

Printed in the United Kingdom by Henry Ling Limited, at the Dorset Press, Dorchester, DT1 1HD

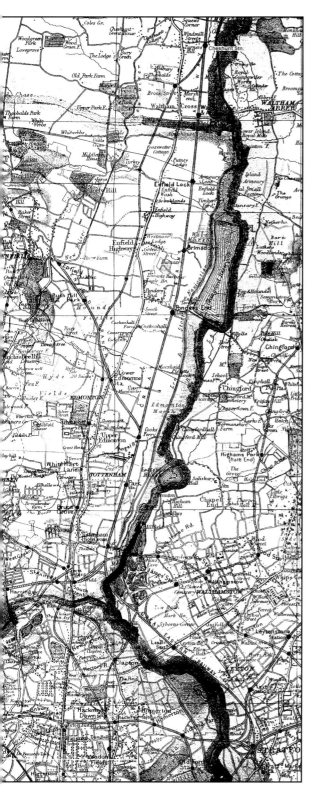

INDEX

ACKNOWLEDGEMENTS

This volume would not have been possible without the assistance of the following gentlemen in addition to the many photographers who have contributed: R. Bradley, B. Bridges, N. Catford, L. Collier, C. Cock (GER Signalling Records), D. Cockle, J. Connor, D. Fairhurst, R. Green, R. Hadingham, F. Hodghton, P. Kay, P. Laming, N. Langridge, P. Paye, the late A. Rush and J. Watling. Also included is my long-suffering wife Belinda, who puts up with my endless chatter about railways and has kindly proof read this work.

We would like to dedicate this album to the memory of Andy Rush, a highly-respected fellow Great Eastern Railway Society member and railwayman, who sadly passed away during the preparation of this album in August 2013. His enormous contribution and lasting legacy was the spreading of GER knowledge.

I. Route diagram in about 1910 (Bacon)

GEOGRAPHICAL SETTING

Following the route of the first main line to Cambridge, we head north from Stratford along the Lea (or Lee) Valley. The River Lea and Lea Navigation eventually flow into the Thames about two miles south of Stratford at Bow Creek and Limehouse Cut. The boundary between Greater London and Essex follows the River Lea and is thus close to the main line. The waterways were once an important artery for the transporting of grain to London. Running south, through Middlesex and bordering Essex, the waterways are separated by large reservoirs as far as Enfield Lock. The main line runs parallel to the waterways, entering Hertfordshire between Enfield Lock and Waltham Cross. Both the Lea Valley Park and Lea Valley Walk provide a 50 mile corridor of recreational activities today. The main line and Southbury Loop mainly traverse alluvium gravel and brick earth. Unless otherwise stated, the maps are to the scale of 25 ins to 1 mile.

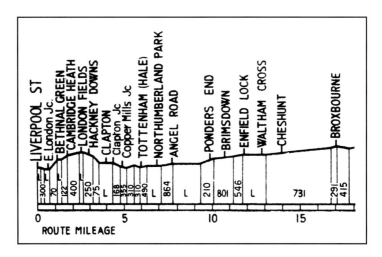

HISTORICAL BACKGROUND

The Eastern Counties Railway opened their station at Stratford on 20th June 1839 when the line from Mile End to Romford opened, built to a gauge of five feet. The Northern & Eastern Railway opened their platforms at Stratford just north-east of the junction on 15th September 1840 when they started running services as far as Broxbourne, along the Lea Valley. To give an idea of how rural the line was at this time, there were a large number of level crossings on the route and only five bridges between Stratford and Broxbourne! The line was extended to Bishops Stortford by 1842 and Cambridge by 1845. In 1844 both lines were converted to standard gauge and the ECR leased the N&ER. The N&ER originally wanted their own terminus at Islington by a shorter route from Tottenham but the cost was prohibitive, hence the connection to the ECR at Stratford. A line south from Stratford to Thames Wharf was opened by the Eastern Counties & Thames Junction Railway in 1846 and extended to North Woolwich a year later. The branch from Edmonton (later Water Lane and even later Angel Road) to Enfield (later Town) opened on 1st March 1849. The line from Stratford, north to Victoria Park, opened in 1854 and the Great Eastern Railway took control of the majority of East Anglian lines in 1862. In 1872 the GER completed both the link from Bethnal Green Junction, Hackney Downs and Clapton to Walthamstow (Hoe Street) and Hackney

Downs to Edmonton (later Lower Edmonton) via Stamford Hill. Walthamstow (Hoe Street) to Chingford opened in 1873.

A marshalling yard was begun at Temple Mills in 1877, just north of Loughton Branch Junction (for Loughton, opening in 1856). The name is derived from an ancient water mill said to have been owned by the Knights Templar. Expansion erupted from 1880 to 1893 to cope with ever greater demand for siding space. In the mid-1950s, the yard had over £3 million spent on it, which resulted in one of the most modern hump shunting yards in the country. This opened officially in 1958 and slowly over the following decades, due to the decline of wagonload freight, especially in the mid-1980s, its fortunes also declined.

The Lea Valley line saw gradual growth in passenger and freight in the Victorian era, evolving over several decades, resulting in large housing estates and hundreds of factories bordering the line. Horticulture and fruit growing became a thriving industry and miles of glasshouses surrounded the line in the Cheshunt area. The GER opened a new double-track line from Bury Street Junction, between Lower Edmonton and Bush Hill Park, to the Cambridge line at Cheshunt on 1st October 1891. Services initially only ran from White Hart Lane (then later Lower Edmonton) to Cheshunt. Lavish stations were built at Churchbury, Forty Hill and Theobalds Grove. The GER had grand plans similar to those in East London, where new stations created wide scale house building and large numbers of new passengers. The plans went awry due to house building not reaching expectations and the introduction of cheap fares on electric trams which paralleled the line to Waltham Cross. By 1907, passenger numbers on the Churchbury loop had declined by half. Theobalds Grove seemed to be the busiest station, as it was nearer to housing development than Cheshunt. By the 1st October 1909 the passenger service, which had only lasted 18 years ceased, despite protests to the House of Commons. World War I provided the line with a brief spell of activity again, brought about by larger numbers of workers required at the Lea Valley armaments and gunpowder factories. In 1915 services were restored to the Churchbury Loop using a steam locomotive powered auto-train and a conductor issuing tickets on the train. The Up line was used for wagon storage and traffic in both directions used the Down line. With the cessation of hostilities in 1918, the passengers evaporated and closure came again on 30th June 1919. The line had a lengthy quiet period after the second closure, with just a daily goods train serving the yards. The station buildings were rented out for local families to live in and lines of washing would be hung out along the platforms. At various times, especially during World War II, the loop was used as a diversionary route when the Lea Valley line was blocked either by engineering works or enemy action. The stored wagons were removed to facilitate double-line working at these times. The rebirth of the Southbury loop came about after the 1954 British Transport Commission Modernisation Plan, when electrification, colour light signalling and track relaying was authorised. Rather than build new stations, the old structures were refurbished with new electric lighting installed. The loop reopened on 21st November 1960 using electric traction. The Lea Valley route from Coppermill Junction to Cheshunt opened to electric trains on the 9th March 1969.

The GER was absorbed by the newly formed London & North Eastern Railway at the 1923 grouping and this passed into the Eastern Region of British Railways at nationalisation in 1948. Passenger services from Stratford to Tottenham Hale ceased on 8th July 1985 and the section of line between Stratford and Coppermill Junction was electrified to aid the flow of freight working in 1989. To improve connections to Cambridge and Stansted Airport, passenger services were reinstated north of Stratford on 12th December 2005. Privatisation saw the lines being rebranded WAGN when Prism Rail was awarded the first franchise on 5th January 1997. Subsequent franchise changes involved National Express from 2004 to 2012, and the lines then became a subsidiary of the Dutch State Railways known as Abellio Greater Anglia. The last of the mechanical signal boxes passed into history on 24th May 2003 when Liverpool Street Integrated Electronic Control Centre (IECC) took control of the signalling on the WAGN routes.

PASSENGER SERVICES

By 1847, trains from London to Cambridge numbered nine on weekdays (5 on Sundays - in brackets henceforth), but only four daily called at Tottenham. There were also 13(6) stopping trains to Broxbourne, mostly destined for Hertford. The 1850 timetable is illustrated and by that time there were 5(3) main line trains also calling at Waltham. By April 1880, there were 9(3) and the local ones are shown in the second table.

The 1910 service involved 31(11) trains to Cheshunt and beyond, 18(11) running via Lea Bridge. Few long distance trains called by that time. Thirty years later, the figures were 34(18) and 11(9). After the first electric trains were introduced, all services (including DMUs) were on regular intervals, usually two per hour via Southbury, one an hour via Brimsdown and one every two hours via Lea Bridge. Some earlier Southbury route timetable samples follow. Later electrifications brought a basic 30-minute interval service on local routes. This also applied when trains were reintroduced north of Stratford, although they were hourly on Sundays.

LONDON, TOTTENHAM, EDMONTON, ENFIELD, WARE, BROXBOURNE and HERTFORD timetable (Week Days and Sundays).

Down timetable — Week Days and Sundays.

NORTHERN AND EASTERN.

London TO Broxbourne.	a.m. 8	10 30 a.m.	1 30	3 30 p.m.	4 30 p.m.	5 30 p.m.	7 30 p.m.	8 30 p.m.	Fares. 1st cls. s. d.	2d cls. s. d.	3d cls. s. d.
Shoreditch	8 0	10 30	1 30	3 30	4 30	5 30	7 30	8 30	1 0	0 9	0 8
Lea Bridge road	8 10	10 40	1 40	3 40	4 40	5 40	7 40	8 40	1 0	0 9	0 8
Tottenham	8 15	10 45	1 45	3 45	4 45	5 45	7 45	8 45	1 0	0 9	0 8
Edmonton	8 20	10 50	1 50	3 50	4 50	..	7 50	8 50	1 0	0 9	0 8
Ponder's End ..	8 25	10 55	1 55	3 55	..	5 55	7 55	8 55	1 6	1 3	1 0
Waltham cross ..	8 30	11 0	2 0	4 0	5 0	6 0	8 0	9 0	2 0	1 6	1 0
Broxbourne ..	8 45	11 15	2 15	4 15	5 15	6 15	8 15	9 15	3 6	2 6	1 6

Broxbourne TO London.	8 15 p.m.	9 a.m.	10 a.m.	12 noon	3 p.m.	5 p.m.	7 p.m.	8	1st cls. s. d.	2d cls. s. d.	3d cls. s. d.
Broxbourne	8 15	9 0	10 0	12 0	3 0	5 0	7 0	8 0	..	..	..
Waltham cross ..	8 20	9 10	10 5	12 5	3 5	5 7	7 5	8 5	1 0	0 9	0 6
Ponder's End ..	8 25	9 10	10 10	12 10	3 10	5 10	7 10	8 10	1 6	1 0	0 9
Edmonton	8 30	..	10 15	12 15	3 15	5 15	7 15	8 15	2 3	1 6	1 0
Tottenham	8 35	9 20	10 20	12 20	3 20	5 20	7 20	8 20	2 6	2 0	1 0
Leabridge road ..	8 45	9 30	10 30	12 30	3 30	5 30	7 30	8 30	2 9	2 0	1 0
Shoreditch	9 0	9 45	10 45	12 45	3 45	5 45	7 45	8 45	3 6	2 6	1 6

On Sundays—From London, 9½, 10½ a.m., 1½, 3½, 5, 30, 5.30 and 8.30 p.m. From Broxbourne, 9 a.m., and 1, 2, 4, 7 and 8 p.m.—stopping at all the stations. Fares for Horses & Carriages.—Private Carriages, 4-wheels, 8s.; ditto 2-wheel 6s.; each. Stage Coaches, 4s. Horses 6s. each.

Bradshaw 1841

August 1862

LIVERPOOL STREET, LOWER EDMONTON, and CHESHUNT.—Great Eastern.

(timetable — Liverpool Street, White Hart Lane, Silver Street, Lower Edmonton, Churchbury, Forty Hill, Theobald's Grove, Cheshunt 152, 153)

March 1909

LIVERPOOL STREET, LOWER EDMONTON, and CHESHUNT.—Great Eastern.

(Down / Week Days / Sundays timetable — Liverpool Street, White Hart Lane, Silver Street, Lower Edmonton, Churchbury, Forty Hill, Theobald's Grove, Cheshunt 316, 317)

January 1916

WHITE HART LANE, LOWER EDMONTON, and CHESHUNT.—Great Eastern.

Week Days only.

(Down timetable — White Hart Lane, Silver Street, Lower Edmonton, Churchbury, Forty Hill, Theobald's Grove, Cheshunt 336, 337)

¶ "Halt" at Carterhatch Lane, for Enfield Highway, between Churchbury and Forty Hill.

Mid-morning extract from May 1968.

					A		C									
LIVERPOOL STREET	d	0842	0852	0902	0912	0922	0936	0942	..	1012	1022	1036	1050	1112	1122	1144	1212	1222
HACKNEY DOWNS	d										28				28			28
CLAPTON	d	50		10		30					31				31			31
STRATFORD	d								1018								1218	
LEA BRIDGE	d								23								23	
TOTTENHAM HALE	d	54		14		34			1027		34				34			1227	34
NORTHUMBERLAND PARK	d	56		16		36					36				36				36
ANGEL ROAD	d	58		18		38					38				38				38
PONDERS END	d	0902		22		42					42				42				42
BRIMSDOWN	d	04		24		44					45				45				45
ENFIELD LOCK	d	07		27		47					47				47				47
WALTHAM CROSS & ABBEY	d	09		29		49					50				50				50
LOWER EDMONTON	d		0907		27		57				27		1106		1201		27		
SOUTHBURY	d		10		30		1000				30		09		04		30		
TURKEY STREET	d		14		34		04				34		13		08		34		
THEOBALDS GROVE	d		17		37		07				37		17		11		37		
CHESHUNT	d	12	19	32	39	0957	09		39		39	1057	18	1157	13		39		1257
BROXBOURNE & HODDESDON	a	0917	24	0937	44		14		44		44		23		18		44		
BROXBOURNE & HODDESDON	d		28		0950		1018		1049			1126		1148		1222		1249	
RYE HOUSE	d		32		54		22		53			30		52		26		53	
ST MARGARET'S	d		35		57		25		56			33		55		29		56	
WARE	d		37		1001		29		1100			37		59		31		1301	
HERTFORD EAST	a		0943		1006		1034		1105			1142		1204		1238		1305	
BROXBOURNE & HODDESDON	d		0926		46		16		46			24		46		20		46	
ROYDON	d		31		51		21		51			29		51		25		51	
HARLOW TOWN	d		35		55		25		55			33		55		29		55	
HARLOW MILL	d		38		58		28		58			36		58		32		58	
SAWBRIDGEWORTH	d		42		1002		32		1102			40		1202		36		1302	
BISHOPS STORTFORD	a		0948		1008		1038		1108			1146		1208		1242		1308	

STRATFORD

1.   Stratford station was originally slightly further east at Angel Lane when the ECR opened in 1839. The N&E platforms were regarded as a separate station when they opened on the Cambridge bound line in 1840. The two stations were combined into one central building (seen here) which opened on 1st April 1847. The station has been rebuilt and expanded several times in its history to become a major interchange. During the 1949 Liverpool Street to Shenfield electrification programme, the Cambridge line platforms were renumbered 11 to 13 and these are where our journey to Cheshunt begins. Today, the Jubilee/Central Lines, Docklands Light Railway, Eurostar (Stratford International), South Eastern (Javelin), Greater Anglia and the London Overground all converge on Stratford, making it one of the busiest stations in the UK. This is Stratford station in 1851, showing the Eastern Counties Railway junction with the Northern & Eastern Railway; left. (ECR Guide)

2.   Stratford Works extension as it appeared shortly after opening in 1847. The Eastern Counties Railway spent over £100,000 constructing the works to move locomotive building from their Romford Factory (now a listed building near Gidea Park). The 1840 Polygon roundhouse had a huge cast ring inside supported by 16 columns. This ring supported a web of wooden roof beams taking the weight of the 132 feet diameter roof. The N&ER built the 16-road Polygon roundhouse, which opened in 1840. The original Stratford Locomotive Works and Carriage Shops on the east side of the Cambridge line evolved from 1840 to 1867. (ECR Guide)

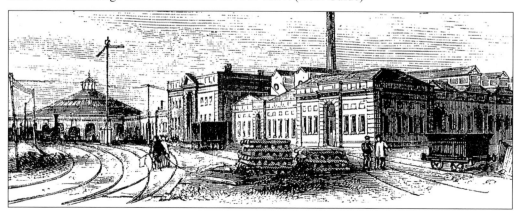

II. 1914 map.

3. The Polygon signal box sitting astride the entrance is seen in 1923 after some alterations. It housed a 24-lever McKenzie & Holland frame with a cleverly designed mechanism under the floor and survived until 4th September 1949 when its duties were handed over to the new Stratford box. (GER)

4. Our journey starts from the Cambridge line Platforms 11 to 13 at Stratford circa 1948. The station area would shortly undergo radical alterations for the electrification of the GE main line. The addition of overhead wires and gantries thereby cluttering any future photographs. The new signal box is nearing completion and in the centre is the Old Yard where much of the rolling stock for Liverpool Street services was marshalled. (J.Searle)

5.   The view north from Platform 11 at nationalisation in 1948. The Polygon roundhouse has been demolished and its associated signal box did not have long to live either. This was the first roundhouse in London and it was a tragedy that it was not saved for future generations to enjoy. There is still a lot of activity around the old works and B12 class 4-6-0 no. 1546 stands under the box minus its tender. The old GER office building stood until 2001. (J.Searle)

6.   This is the view looking north adjacent to Stratford station signal box in 1960. To the left is the Old Yard with both 03 and 08 class diesel shunters being kept busy by the constant marshalling of vans and passenger stock. The wonderful GER canopies with their ornate spandrels and supporting columns were unceremoniously demolished in 1977 leaving an abandoned, barren and overgrown island platform behind. Latterly, only platform 11 on the right escaped demolition. (J.E.Connor coll.)

7.   The massive redevelopment of Stratford station to cope with the sheer numbers of visitors to the 2012 Olympics also coincided with a vast new shopping centre occupying much of the old locomotive depot site. Here we see class 378 EMU no. 211 with a London Overground Richmond bound service on 1st July 2011. To the right can be seen a class 317 EMU on a Bishops Stortford service on the site of the original platform 11 seen in the previous view. The massive footbridge is not for passenger use and carries customers into the shopping centre. (A.Grimmett)

For other views of this area, see Middleton Press albums:
Liverpool Street to Ilford
Branch Lines around North Woolwich
Branch Line to Ongar
St. Pancras to Folkestone

NORTH OF STRATFORD

8.   This view is of Chobham Farm Junction looking towards Stratford on 28th May 1922. The box was abolished on 29/6/58 when its duties were taken over by the new Temple Mills East box. The massive carriage works dominates the left hand side and to the right we see the main access for locomotives going to and from the engine sheds, which fan out in the murky gloom and constant fog that pervaded the site. Also on the right can be seen Loop Junction signal box, controlling the pair of tracks that bisected the depot to Fork Junction. As this was the largest engine shed in the country, it is ironic that Stratford today does not possess even a single siding for locomotives, but it does have the Eurostar depot. (GER)

GREAT EASTERN RAILWAY
Not transferable. Issued subject to Regulations in the Company's Time Tables.
5232   LEA BRIDGE to   5232
Lea Bridge   Lea Bridge
STRATFORD
Stratford   Stratford
2d.   2d.
THIRD CLASS
Available on day of issue only.

GREAT EASTERN RAILWAY
Not transferable. Issued subject to Regulations in the Company's Time Tables.
6398   TOTTENHAM to   6398
Tottenham   Tottenham
STRATFORD
Stratford   Stratford
3d.   FARE   3d.
Third Class
Available on day of issue only.

STRATFORD DEPOT

II. This was the layout of the Polygon Engine House in 1840. Whilst locomotive repairs and storage to the east of the main line proved adequate in the early years, as the railway system grew it became very cramped. After the GER took control of loco operations in 1862, there were discussions about expansion for several years until they purchased land just west of the station on what was part of Hackney Marsh and opened the New Shed in 1871. Soon overtaken by continuing growth of its services, there was further demand for covered loco sheds and the 12-road Jubilee Shed holding 60 locos opened in 1887. Stratford Works produced over 1700 locomotives prior to 1924 when the last loco constructed there, left the works. In the mid-1950s over 2500 workers were employed around the shed which had gained the shed code of 30A. A very large workshop known as the High Meads Engine Repair Shop (Diesel Repair Shop in later years) opened during the World War I. The whole complex became the largest engine shed in the country and its demise in 2001 was viewed with great sadness by thousands of former workers and enthusiasts. Apart from a small section of the old loco works perimeter wall in Leyton Road, nothing remains.

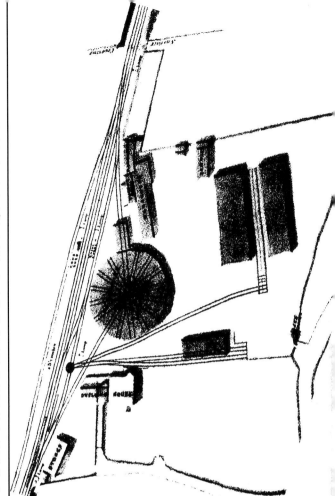

). Prior to the opening of the diesel depot, some of the earliest main line diesel arrivals at Stratford were the Class 40 English Electric Type 4s for the Norwich services in 1958. This rare picture shows one such locomotive from the first batch D200 – D205 standing outside the Jubilee shed in late 1958. The Class 40s ousted the Britannia class steam locomotives in this year, but their performance was little better than the Britannia's. A Buckjumper 0-6-0T shunts a B1 and some of its classmates out of the shed. (Author's coll.)

10.   The early 1960s provided visitors to Stratford depot with the short-lived sight of both the steam and diesel sheds standing side by side. The segregation was important for the maintenance of diesel locomotives which required a much cleaner environment. Class 15 and 16 Bo-Bo Type 1 diesels stand guard outside their territory, whilst a variety of steam locomotives rather poignantly cling to life around the old Jubilee shed and the coal stage on the right. (Transport Treasury)

11.   Looking towards Stratford from Temple Mills Lane bridge in 1954, we see just some of the vastness that was Stratford loco depot, much of which is covered in the familiar sulphurous fog, which seemed to permanently hang over the whole area. Several steam engines are busy fighting for space in the bottleneck here. This was the main entry and exit point for the depot. The road crossing on the right gave access to the depot for vehicles. (Author's coll.)

↓ 12. After the Jubilee shed was demolished in the early 1960s, the roads on the left were numbered 3, 4 and 5 Steam Roads for the rest of the depot's days. We have a superb view taken in 1970 showing the B and C Running Sheds surrounded by the traction of the day including a row of class 15 BTH Bo-Bo diesels, which were all withdrawn by March 1971. Fortunately, one example survives and can be found on the East Lancs Railway. In the background is the vast Stratford International Freight Terminal. (J.Searle)

TEMPLE MILLS
MARSHALLING
YARD

IV.   The top map is from 1946 and is scaled at 2" to 1 mile. A siding was first recorded here in 1877 and gradual expansion over the following two decades saw the evolution of a ramshackle system of eight separate yards causing much short-hop trip working between them. In the late 1950s, over a four year period, the yard was totally rebuilt to become the most modern automated hump shunting yard of its day. Over 50 sorting sidings could handle thousands of wagons every day. During the rebuilding, the main line was diverted from the middle of the yard around the west side. There was also a large wagon works here from 1896 onwards, which employed over 800 men at its peak. The yards declined during the mid-1980s and became derelict. It was redeveloped over a period of several years to become a major servicing centre for Eurostar trains, opening in 2007. At the northern end of the yard, a new yard for electric units known as Orient Way opened in 2008, replacing the old Thornton Field sidings near Stratford, which were in the way of the Olympic stadium.

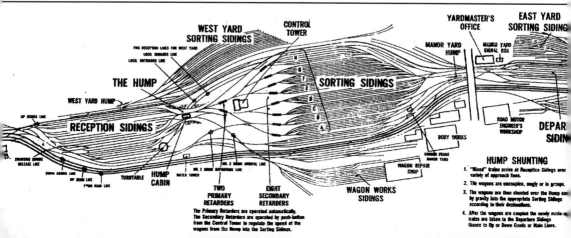

HUMP SHUNTING

1. "Mixed" trains arrive at Reception Sidings over variety of approach lines.

2. The wagons are uncoupled, singly or in groups.

3. The wagons are then shunted over the Hump and by gravity into the appropriate Sorting Sidings according to their destinations.

4. After the wagons are coupled the newly made-up trains are taken to the Departure Sidings thence to Up or Down Goods or Main Lines.

13. Temple Mills South box once stood close to Ruckholt Road bridge and the site of its replacement, Manor Yard box. The new Temple Mills East box also took over some of the operations in 1958. The box opened in 1881 and closed in 1957, when the yard was being modernised. (Unknown)

14. The iconic Temple Mills Marshalling Control Tower is seen in January 1959. The yard had been rebuilt at a cost of over £3 million and opened in September 1958. The building underneath the control tower housed compressors which supplied air to the mechanical wagon retarders in the foreground. (BR)

← 15.   Looking south in 1960 from the water tower in Temple Mills loco depot, we see ROD class 01 2-8-0 no. 63678 running light engine from the loco sidings, as it heads underneath the Hump Cabin where class J20 0-6-0 no. 64689 passes by. The Hump Cabin controller would set the route for each wagon passing over the hump and instructions on where to uncouple were given to the shunter on the ground. In the background, an 08 diesel shunting loco can be seen in the West Yard. (BR)

← 16.   Looking north in the opposite direction towards Lea Bridge Gas Works in 1960, we see the coaling plant and turntable, with two steam engines waiting their next turn of duty. The loco servicing depot here saved a lot of light engine movements to and from Stratford depot, which was hard pressed at times to accommodate the volume of traffic. The Hump Reception roads are unusually quiet. Two pairs of 08 diesels were employed to push the trains over the hump day and night. (BR)

17.   This is the view from the top of the Hump reception roads looking north towards Lea Bridge in 1961, shortly after the new Temple Mills diesel shed had opened. A class 16 Bo-Bo diesel stands outside the shed, which was still equipped with a turntable and coaling plant for visiting steam engines. (Author's coll.)

18.   Class J69/1 0-6-0T no. 68542 takes on water outside Temple Mills East signal box on 1st June 1962. Within just three months, scenes like this in East London would disappear, with the abolition of steam from East Anglia. This Stratford allocated engine was withdrawn shortly afterwards. One of the last ever steam workings into Temple Mills was on 24th November 1966, when two troop trains hauled by Southern 4-6-2s, numbers 34013 *Okehampton* and 34023 *Blackmore Vale* arrived from Southampton. The ER soon replaced them with diesels for their onward journeys into East Anglia. (L.Sandler)

19.　　Ex-LMS 0-6-0T 3F class no. 47611 approaches Ruckholt Road bridge with a freight off the London Midland Region on 25th November 1961. The sheer scale of the yard and the tremendous amount of activity is evident. The main yard had 49 double-ended sidings and could handle thousands of wagons per day. (B.W.L.Brooksbank/Initial Photos)

20.　　A class 33 Birmingham Railway & Wagon Company Type 3 Bo-Bo no. 33039 enters the yard at Temple Mills West with a freight off the Southern Region. The hump reception roads and surroundings are dominated by the monolithic appearance of Lea Bridge Gas Works in the background. A pair of 08 shunting locos wait to push the wagons over the hump. Temple Mills West signal box closed in 1988 and the yard became sombre, neglected and overgrown. (P.Groom)

LEA BRIDGE

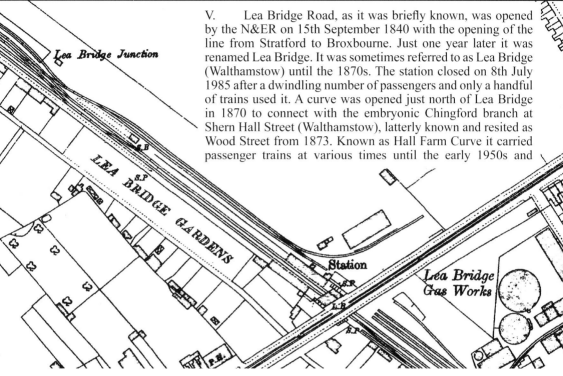

V.   Lea Bridge Road, as it was briefly known, was opened by the N&ER on 15th September 1840 with the opening of the line from Stratford to Broxbourne. Just one year later it was renamed Lea Bridge. It was sometimes referred to as Lea Bridge (Walthamstow) until the 1870s. The station closed on 8th July 1985 after a dwindling number of passengers and only a handful of trains used it. A curve was opened just north of Lea Bridge in 1870 to connect with the embryonic Chingford branch at Shern Hall Street (Walthamstow), latterly known and resited as Wood Street from 1873. Known as Hall Farm Curve it carried passenger trains at various times until the early 1950s and thereafter just freight and empty stock trains would keep the rails polished. When the Chingford line was electrified in 1960, the curve had overhead equipment installed, but electric trains never travelled over it and the track was lifted in 1967. The map is dated 1913.

21.   This is a view dating from the 1890s showing the mainly wooden building and gas lighting on the up road platform as we look towards Copper Mill Junction. Faintly at the far end of the platform is Lea Bridge Junction signal box which opened in 1880 replacing an earlier cabin. Two goods lines were added behind the station in the 1930s. (P.Laming coll.)

22.   This is the very ornate exterior of Lea Bridge on the north side of Lea Bridge Road as it appeared in 1897. The building was designed by the architect Sancton Wood (1815-1886), who also designed Cambridge, Ipswich and Bury St. Edmunds stations. It had a bell turret on the roof, which was rung to tell passengers that a train was due. (J.E.Connor coll.)

23.   The building was damaged in World War II and survived minus its roof until the early 1960s when it was demolished. The shell is seen here in 1948 looking somewhat forlorn and still sporting its LNER signage. The once-ornate windows have been replaced by iron railings. There is evidence in the brickwork, that the stairways once had canopies. A very plain and rather austere replacement was built on the site. (LNER/BR)

24.   A North Woolwich to Palace Gates service formed of ex-LNER quint-art coaches approaches Lea Bridge in March 1957. The train is hauled by N7 class 0-6-2T no. 69715. (B.Pask)

25.   J15 class 0-6-0 no. 65361 waits for the signal outside Lea Bridge Gas Works in 1957 with a northbound freight from Temple Mills. These locos were remarkable survivors from a bygone era at this time. Built by the GER from 1883, there were eventually 289 in the class and 127 survived into the BR period. The final four were withdrawn in September 1962 and only one (no. 65462) survives in preservation. (B.Pask)

26.   Although the quality is not good, this is a rare view of Lea Bridge signal box just prior to closure. The box succumbed on the 20th April 1958, when its duties were acquired by the new Temple Mills West box and it was demolished shortly afterwards. We are looking north towards Copper Mill Junction and BR dark blue enamel totem signs are affixed to some of the lamp posts. (J.E.Connor coll.)

27.   A J17 0-6-0 tender loco passes through the station with a mixed freight in the late 1950s. The signal box is located just behind the tender. Much industry built up around the station and in the distance is the former AEC bus and railcar factory, which was relocated to Southall in the mid-1920s. The trackwork here appears to be rather alarming, but this effect has been caused by a ripple on the original photo. (Walthamstow Pump House Museum coll.)

28.   Early in 1962 we see antique J15 class 0-6-0 no. 65465 storming past Lea Bridge Gas Works with a train of condemned wagons entering Temple Mills yard from the north. The connection for the gas works was severed in 1968. (G.Silcock)

29.   The forlorn, unloved and scruffy buildings would have been more at home on an allotment than a railway station. This is how poor Lea Bridge appeared in the mid-1970s. The old 1950s BR dark blue enamel totem sign gives some indication that the station had been more highly thought of in the past. Our view is towards the Temple Mills hump yard in the distance. (J.E.Connor coll.)

30. Class 31 Brush Type 2 diesel no. 31190 passes Lea Bridge on the up goods line as it approaches Temple Mills with an empty coal train on 14th May 1979. To the right is the parcels depot which was still just about in use. There was also an extensive goods yard to the right, but this had been closed since 1970. (www.TOPticl.com)

31. This is the last train on the last day of BR services on 8th July 1985. The two-car Cravens Class 105 DMU arrives from Tottenham Hale on its way to Stratford and carries a headboard to commemorate the occasion. The goods lines which once carried large numbers of freight trains for Temple Mills are rusty and becoming overgrown. A new station was planned for 2014. (A.Grimmett)

COPPER MILL JUCTION

VI. The 1915 extract is at 15 ins to the mile.

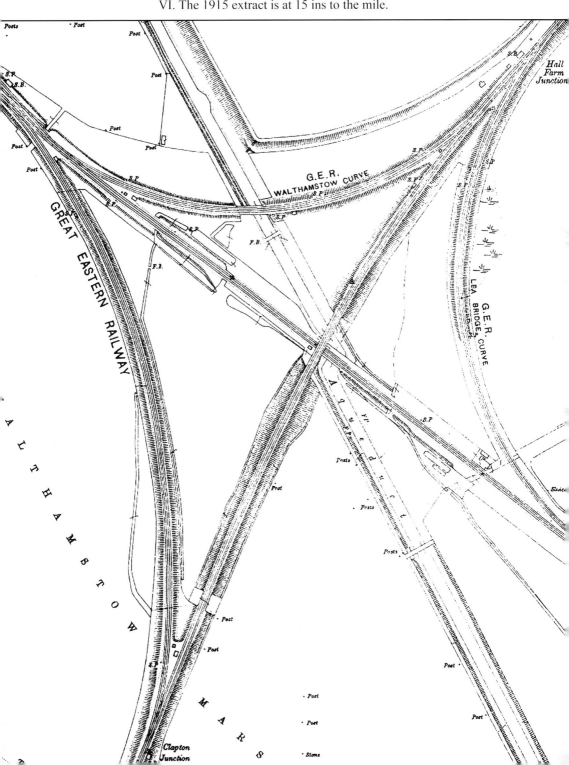

32.　　　This view looking north towards Tottenham shows Copper Mill Junction as it appeared in 1911. From left to right the lines are from Clapton Junction and Liverpool Street, with the centre tracks leading to Lea Bridge then Stratford and on the right is the curve to the Chingford line at Hall Farm Junction, which was closed on 11th June 1960. A pair of freight only lines were added to the right in the early 1930s and the junction was remodelled. (GER)

33.　　　With the lines to Copper Mill Junction appearing from the left and the lines to Clapton in the middle, plus the curve sweeping down to Lea Bridge Junction on the right, this is a rare view of Hall Farm Junction on the Chingford line during the GER period. The date is 1911 and both curves would have seen regular use at this time. The signal box closed on 29th January 1938, when its duties were taken over by Clapton Junction during installation of colour light signals on the Chingford line. (GER)

34.   To complete the trio of junctions around Copper Mill, we are looking east from Clapton Junction signal box on the Chingford line in 1911. This box was only two years old at this time, replacing an earlier structure. Photos of this junction were not available for the Liverpool Street to Chingford volume, so it is appropriate to include them here. Copper Mill Junction is to the far left. (GER)

35.   With the lonely Hackney Marshes as a backdrop, we are looking at Clapton Junction signal box as it appeared in 1959, just before the overhead wires were installed for the Chingford electrification. The box was damaged by a bomb on 11th February 1945, hence the brick base surround. It closed on 22nd May 1960, some six months before the electric service started. (Author's coll.)

36.   N7 class 0-6-2T no. 69652 passes over Copper Mill Junction with a North Woolwich to Palace Gates service in about 1960. New colour light signals are about to replace the semaphores. The Chingford line is carried on the bridge in the background, whilst Hall Farm curve rises on a steep gradient to the left to join it. Clapton Junction is just out of view to the right. (Author's coll.)

37.   Ministry of Supply War Department "Austerity" class 2-8-0 no. 90474 passes Copper Mill Junction signal box with a freight heading towards Temple Mills during the early 1950s. Over 700 of these powerful freight engines were built from 1943 onwards and BR purchased them in 1948. Copper Mill Junction box was taken out of use in February 1969, when its duties were taken over by Temple Mills West box. (A.G.Ellis)

38.   Class 25 Type 2 Sulzer Bo-Bo no. D7523 spins her wheels as she struggles to accelerate a heavy train for Cricklewood, after having been brought to a stand just before Copper Mill Junction on the 9th June 1969. The Chingford line passes on the bridge behind the loco. By a strange coincidence, D7523 (25173) became one of the last members of the class in service and now resides on the Epping Ongar Railway, located just a few miles away. (P.H.Groom)

39.   Class 43 Warship no. D856 Trojan in BR blue livery passes Copper Mill Junction with a freight for Temple Mills in June 1970. The WR hydraulics sometimes strayed from their Paddington and West Country haunts and visited Temple Mills. They occasionally ventured even further into ER territory at Ripple Lane (Barking). This locomotive was withdrawn in May 1971 and was cut up shortly afterwards. (P.H.Groom)

40.   Class 308/3 3-car EMU no. 455 approaches Copper Mill Junction with the 14.57 Hertford East to Liverpool Street service on 5th June 1970. These units (453 – 455) were almost identical to the 305/1 units 401 – 452, which had a first class section, but they were built in 1961 with second class seating only. In the BR period, the junction was referred to as Coppermill Junction. (P.H.Groom)

Extracts from *Bradshaw's Guide 1866*
as seen on TV (reprinted by Middleton Press).

STRATFORD.
POPULATION, 15,994.
A telegraph station.
HOTEL.—The Swan.
OMNIBUSES to and from London every five minutes.
This station forms an important junction of the lines to Cambridge, Ipswich, Tilbury, and places on the North London Railway. Here a collier dock of 600 acres is being constructed. At West Ham are distilleries, Gutta Percha factories, and the gate of an abbey.

TOTTENHAM.
POPULATION, 13,240.
Distance from station, 1 mile.
A telegraph station.
HOTEL.—White Hart.
The collection of Turner's drawings, &c., belonging to the late F. Windus, Esq., can be viewed on Mondays. The Hermitage, near the old wooden cross, was Izaak Walton's delight. Bruce Castle (a school kept by the Messrs. Hill), stands on the site of a house which belonged to King Robert Bruce's father.

41.   A class 317/2 EMU no. 372 approaches the junction with a Liverpool Street bound service on the 5th April 1990. These secondhand units have been used on WAGN services for many years, having started life on the Kings Cross – Peterborough route in 1987. The very first 317/1 units date back to 1983 and the newly electrified St. Pancras – Bedford route. The trackbed of the former down goods loop can be seen on the left. (P.H.Groom)

42.   The class 315 units form the backbone of the Liverpool Street to Hertford East, Chingford and Enfield Town services. Here we see unit no. 828 heading towards London with such a service on 24th May 1990. Large reservoirs envelop the line on either side. These units date from 1980 and are shared with those on the Liverpool Street, Gidea Park and Shenfield services. (P.H.Groom)

TOTTENHAM HALE

VII.   The station was opened by the Northern & Eastern Railway as Tottenham on 15th September 1840, when the line to Broxbourne opened. It was rebuilt in 1859 and renamed Tottenham Hale by the Great Eastern Railway in 1875 (although curiously, the Hale suffix was not show on tickets). It again reverted back to plain Tottenham under the LNER in 1938 and finally Tottenham Hale once more with the opening on the Victoria Line in 1968. The 1894 edition map is at 15ins to the mile.

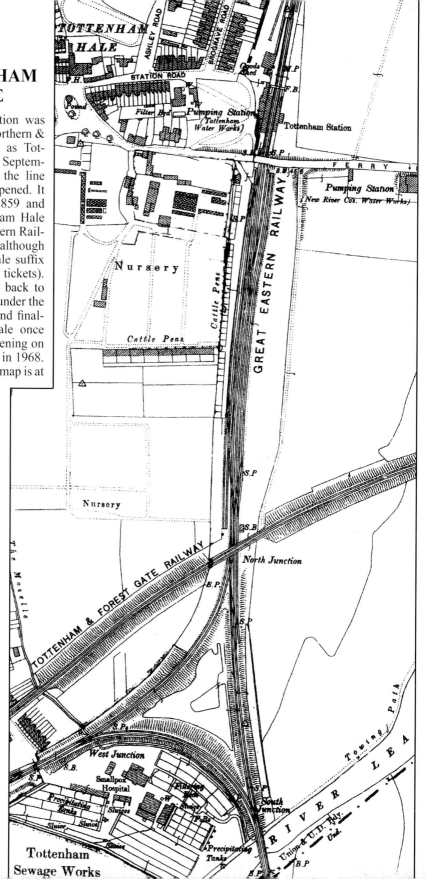

43.   An early 1900s view shows GER class Y14 (LNER J15) 0-6-0 tender engine no. 627, which was relatively new at this time, being built at Stratford in 1884, heading south through the station towards Temple Mills. (P.Laming coll.)

44.   Tottenham West Junction is seen here in 1961 and formed part of the former 'Tottenham Triangle', as it was known by railwaymen. The junction formed a useful link for freight off the Tottenham & Hampstead line onto the Lea Valley line. In this view looking east we can see the connection on the left leading to Tottenham North Junction (curve closed 14/5/61) and the curve on the right leading to Tottenham South and Copper Mill Junctions. (R.Hadingham coll.)

45. This is Tottenham West Junction, looking west in 1961. Trains off the Southern Region, particularly troop trains, would have the steam locomotive replaced by an E engine here. The SR engine could then be turned on the triangle before heading home. The north curve was also used by GER passenger services to and from St. Pancras. The box was opened by the GER in 1880 and closed on 27th July 1963. (R.Hadingham coll.)

6. We have an interior view f Tottenham South Junction gnal box, looking towards oppermill Junction in 1961. he signalman is Charles adingham, the photographer's ther. The GER box opened in 899 and contained a Saxby Farmer No. 9 Duplex 31-ver frame. It closed on 17th ebruary 1969. R.Hadingham coll.)

47. A view looking north from Tottenham South Junction signal box in 1957 as class N7 0-6-2T no. 69623 heading towards Temple Mills with a short freight on the main line. The curve to the left heads towards South Tottenham station and the bridge carrying the Tottenham & Hampstead line can be seen in the distance. (R.Hadingham coll.)

48.   N7 class 0-6-2T no. 69688 calls at Tottenham with a northbound service on 20th July 1954. A trolleybus can be seen on the Ferry Road bridge in the background. The goods shed is on the right. Goods traffic ceased here in 1968. (A.A.Jackson)

49.   In November 1959, BR named one of its new express freight trains which served centres of fruit and vegetable traffic as the Lea Valley Enterprise. The train started from Tottenham then picked up at Angel Road, Ponders End, Brimsdown, Waltham Cross and Broxbourne and ran non-stop to Whitemoor (March) for onward delivery to the North. The train was often double-headed by class 31 diesels and the driver of one such train is seen here proudly placing the headboard on the front of his charge.
(R.Hadingham coll.)

50.   A Lea Valley 6-car class 125 Rolls Royce engined DMU set creates a haze of exhaust fumes as it accelerates away from Tottenham Hale on 11th July 1967 with a Cheshunt to Stratford service. The old up side yard is very overgrown due to the decline in Lea Valley freight traffic, but the goods lines are clinging to life on the far right. (P.H.Groom)

51.　　Today's railway lacks variety when it comes to loco-hauled freight services. This was not the case in the early 1970s, when there were frequent surprise appearances from other regions. Here we see Class 52 Type 4 diesel hydraulic no. D1056 *Western Sultan* entering the curve at Tottenham South Junction with a freight from Temple Mills during August 1974, bound for the Western Region. (N.L.Cadge)

52.　　A Liverpool Street to Stansted Airport service calls on 31st July 2013, in the shape of class 379 Electrostar no. 021. These state of the art units built at Derby, were introduced in March 2011 on Stansted and Cambridge services. They have CCTV cameras on the roof to monitor the pantograph. The DOO system uses bodyside cameras with in-cab monitors for the driver. (Author)

NORTHUMBERLAND PARK

VIII.   Just two years after the initial N&ER line had opened from Stratford to Broxbourne, a station was opened with the name Marsh Lane on 1st April 1842. It was renamed Park on the 1st June 1852 by the ECR. In 1923, the LNER came into existence and bestowed the title of Northumberland Park on the station from the 1st July. Adjacent to the east side of the station was a large 14-road marshalling yard. The yard closed in the 1960s and the site was purchased by London Underground for the Victoria Line depot. The 1893 map is scaled at 25 ins to the mile.

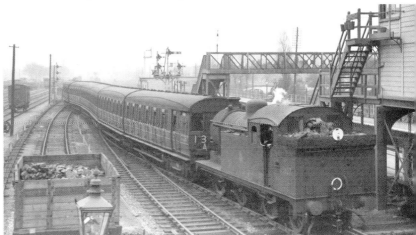

53.   With Tottenham Hotspur's White Hart Lane football stadium being less than a ten minute walk away, many football specials used Northumberland Park in order to relieve the pressure on White Hart Lane. Having arrived from Chingford via Hall Farm Curve with such a special, class N7 0-6-2T no. 69627 is propelling its empty stock into the up sidings ready for the return working during April 1958. (B.Pask)

54.   Looking north in 1955 we witness a class D16/3 4-4-0 standing by Northumberland Park marshalling yard's water tower. The 17 road yard was used mainly as an overflow yard to relieve the pressure on Temple Mills during busy periods, where lengthy trains from the north could be remarshalled. An early Drewry 0-6-0 diesel shunting loco stands by for its next duty and a class N7 0-6-2T heads past with a Hertford East service. The station with its distinctive tall signal box can be seen in the distance. (Author's coll.)

55.   On the 23rd November 1967, we witness class 15 BTH/Paxman Type 1 Bo-Bo no. D8200 heading north with the 09.42 Stratford to Broxbourne parcels train. The view is taken from the signal box and shows that the station still has gas lighting. (P.Paye)

November 1865

LONDON, ENFIELD, BROXBOURNE, WARE, BUNTINGFORD, and HERTFORD.—Great Eastern.

56.　A Stratford bound 6-car Derby-built class 125 DMU passes the Victoria Line depot on 13th June 1968. Construction of the new underground line began in 1962 and the first section from Walthamstow to Highbury opened on 1st September 1968, with the section to Victoria following in March 1969. The sidings which once bordered the main line have all but disappeared. (P.H.Groom)

57.　Here we see the station on 3rd December 1970, shortly after the line had been electrified. The old brick built station building has been replaced by a somewhat less attractive modern edifice, whilst the up side platform has a very unsightly bus shelter acting as a last resort to protect passengers from the cold, wind and rain! There is an odd combination of the old and new, with the signal box, level crossing and platform benches firmly harking back to a bygone era. (B.Pask)

58.   The unusual lofty signal box dated from 1914 when the goods lines were added. It was a McKenzie & Holland box, latterly with a 54-lever frame. As the marshalling yard and goods lines disappeared in the late 1960s, its role was diminished. From 1969 its main function was to control the level crossing as seen here on 19th April 1984. On 24th April 1988 the box was made redundant by CCTV cameras overlooking Marsh Lane crossing, monitored from Brimsdown. In 2002 even this function was superseded by Liverpool Street IECC taking over. It is noteworthy that the BR(E) dark blue enamel name is still in place. (P.Kay)

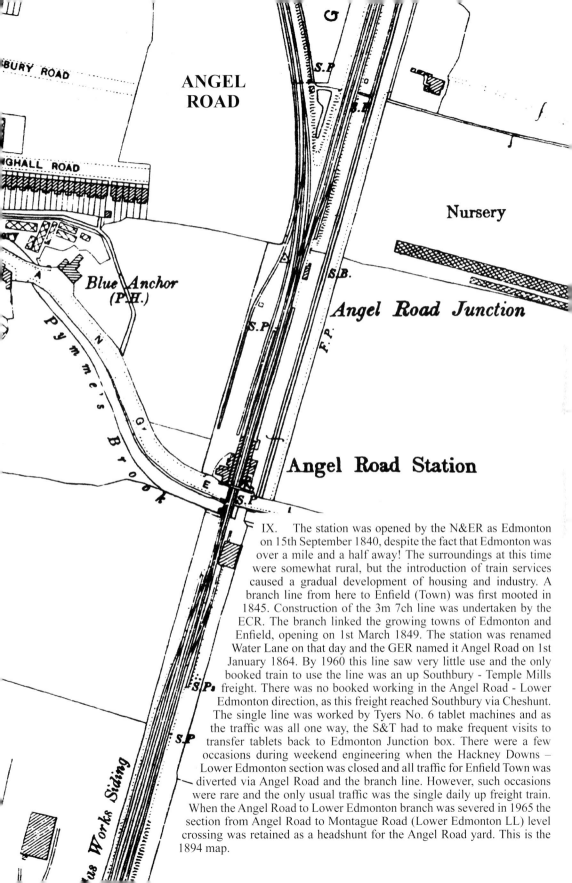

ANGEL ROAD

Nursery

Blue Anchor (P.H.)

Angel Road Junction

Angel Road Station

IX.   The station was opened by the N&ER as Edmonton on 15th September 1840, despite the fact that Edmonton was over a mile and a half away! The surroundings at this time were somewhat rural, but the introduction of train services caused a gradual development of housing and industry. A branch line from here to Enfield (Town) was first mooted in 1845. Construction of the 3m 7ch line was undertaken by the ECR. The branch linked the growing towns of Edmonton and Enfield, opening on 1st March 1849. The station was renamed Water Lane on that day and the GER named it Angel Road on 1st January 1864. By 1960 this line saw very little use and the only booked train to use the line was an up Southbury - Temple Mills freight. There was no booked working in the Angel Road - Lower Edmonton direction, as this freight reached Southbury via Cheshunt. The single line was worked by Tyers No. 6 tablet machines and as the traffic was all one way, the S&T had to make frequent visits to transfer tablets back to Edmonton Junction box. There were a few occasions during weekend engineering when the Hackney Downs – Lower Edmonton section was closed and all traffic for Enfield Town was diverted via Angel Road and the branch line. However, such occasions were rare and the only usual traffic was the single daily up freight train. When the Angel Road to Lower Edmonton branch was severed in 1965 the section from Angel Road to Montague Road (Lower Edmonton LL) level crossing was retained as a headshunt for the Angel Road yard. This is the 1894 map.

59.   We look north at Angel Road Junction in 1911 as an up road goods train waits patiently in the loop for a fast train to pass. The signal box was relatively new at this time, being opened in 1909 to replace an earlier structure. It had a 45 lever frame, controlling the main lineand loops. The junction to Lower Edmonton Low Level can be seen diverging to the left near the uncluttered goods yard. The box was closed on 9th March 1969 when the main line was electrified. (J. Watling coll./GER)

60. This is a view of Angel Road looking south in the early 1960s towards the gas works on the right. The Tottenham & Edmonton Gas Light & Coke Company was producing gas here by 1847 and production continued up to 1972. There was a level crossing at this point before the road bridge was built. The station retained many of its original features, signage and canopies until the electrification of the Lea Valley line in 1969. (B.Pask)

61.   Another early 1960s view looks north towards the junction. The signal is off for the main line and the branch signal is to the left. The signal box is out of view. The goods lines pass behind the up road platform on the right. (J.E.Connor coll.)

LONDON, TOTTENHAM, WALTHAM CROSS, BROXBOURNE, ST. MARGARET'S, and HERTFORD.—Great Eastern.

Down — Week Days

Down.							
Liverpool Street...dep.							
Bishopsgate							
Bethnal Green							
London Fields							
Hackney Downs Junc.							
Clapton							
Globe Road *							
Coborn Rd. for Old Ford							
Stratford							
Lea Bridge							
St. Pancras...dep.							
Kentish Town							
South Tottenham							
Tottenham (Hale)							
Park							
Angel Road							
Lower Edmonton 198							
Ponder's End							
Brimsdown							
Enfield Lock ‡ Abbey							
Waltham Cross and							
Cheshunt 201							
Broxbourne § 170 {arr. / dep.							
Rye House							
St. Margaret's 173.							
Ware ‖231							
Hertford (Railway St.) ‖							

Down—Continued. Week Days—Continued. Sundays.

a Slip Carriage detached at 2 39 aft.   b Runs 23 minutes later on Saturdays.   c Arrives at St. Pancras at 2 50 aft.   e Saturdays only.

December 1895

62.   A Ripple Lane (Barking) to Whitemoor (March) freight is hauled by a pair class 31 Brush Type 2 diesels (D5624 and D5635) and heads north through Angel Road on 9th November 1963. In the foreground is the branch connection to Lower Edmonton Low Level, which closed just over a year later. (P.Paye)

63.   This view shows the former junction to Lower Edmonton Low Level just after the main line connection had been severed in 1965. A new connection off the down main line was added later, to access the yard. Network Rail has come under increasing pressure from local rail users and the council for a third running line between Lea Bridge and Brimsdown. (Author's coll.)

64.   Looking north in about 1970 during track relaying we see a class 15 Bo-Bo 800 H.P. diesel passing on the goods line, which once ran all the way to Picketts Lock, but by this time had been reduced to a single line worked in both directions. It can be seen to rejoin the main line just north of the station and there is still a connection to the goods yard where the former junction diverged. (B.Brockbank)

GREAT EASTERN RAILWAY
Not transferable. Issued subject to Regulations
in the Company's Time Tables.
0353   CHESHUNT   to   0353
Cheshunt   Cheshunt
Enfield L [FORENFIELD WASH] Enfield L
ENFIELD LOCK
2d.   FARE   2d.
Third Class
Available on day of issue only.

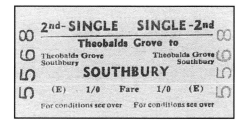

2nd- SINGLE   SINGLE -2nd
5568   **Theobalds Grove** to   5568
Theobalds Grove   Theobalds Grove
Southbury   Southbury
SOUTHBURY
(E)   1/0   Fare   1/0   (E)
For conditions see over   For conditions see over

PONDERS END

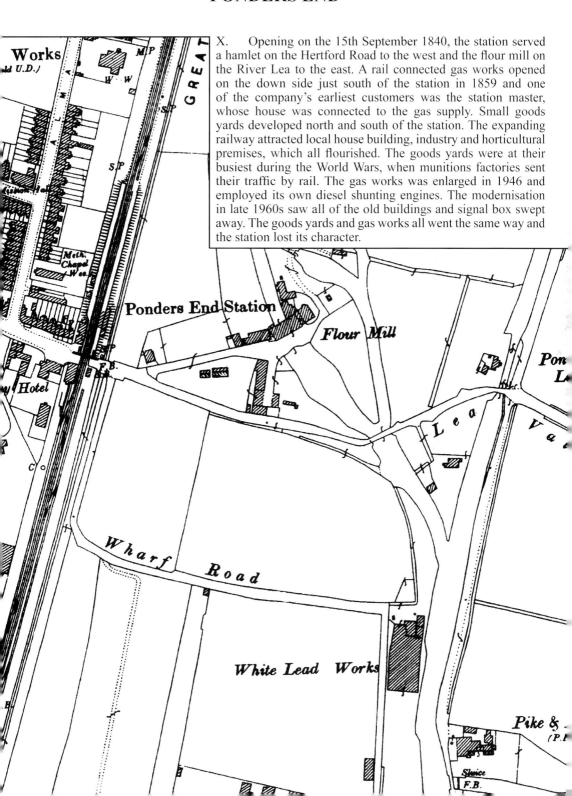

X.   Opening on the 15th September 1840, the station served a hamlet on the Hertford Road to the west and the flour mill on the River Lea to the east. A rail connected gas works opened on the down side just south of the station in 1859 and one of the company's earliest customers was the station master, whose house was connected to the gas supply. Small goods yards developed north and south of the station. The expanding railway attracted local house building, industry and horticultural premises, which all flourished. The goods yards were at their busiest during the World Wars, when munitions factories sent their traffic by rail. The gas works was enlarged in 1946 and employed its own diesel shunting engines. The modernisation in late 1960s saw all of the old buildings and signal box swept away. The goods yards and gas works all went the same way and the station lost its character.

Works
ld U.D.)

Meth.
Chapel
Wes.

Ponders End Station

Flour Mill

Pon
L

Lea   Va

Hotel

Wharf   Road

White Lead Works

Pike &
(P.F

Sluice
F.B.

65.   We are looking north towards Brimsdown in what is quite clearly a GER view. The ticket office, with its unusual arched roof, and the station masters house, date from the opening of the line in 1840. (P.Laming coll.)

66.   English Electric class 37 Co-Co no. D6716 (37016) speeds through the station with a Kings Lynn to Liverpool Street express in October 1967. This was a Stratford (30A) based loco at this time and the class was the most commonly used diesel class for express passenger trains on this route for over 20 years. Carrying BR green with half yellow warning panels, this was the most attractive livery to adorn the class. (D.Fairhurst)

67.   This rather delightful view is of the signal box and goods shed, looking north in 1967. The buildings are covered in a coating of light brown brake dust accumulated over many decades, giving the atmosphere of a bygone era. The box dates from 1879 and closed in January 1969. There was a trailing connection off the down main to the gas works (out of view) which was severed in 1971. (D.Fairhurst)

68. The signal box is just visible on the right in this 1967 view of the site of the old South Street level crossing, looking east. The road, originally just a country lane became the A110 in 1919 and long queues of traffic resulted in demands for a bridge. Closure of the level crossings was brought about by a new A110 bridge north of the station which opened in 1963. (D.Fairhurst)

69. On the 13th September 1960 Brush Type 2 Class 31 no. D5572 came to grief with the 04.45 Temple Mills to Peterborough. No less than 18 wagons and the loco became spectacularly derailed at Picketts Lock, seen here looking south. Many services were diverted via the Churchbury loop whilst the clean up took place and a DMU shuttle operated between Cheshunt and Ponders End. From the south, a shuttle ran between Angel Road and Stratford. The up and down Goods lines from Angel Road to Picketts Lock closed in 1967 and Picketts Lock box closed on 9th March 1969. The box had been known as Pickards and Picketts Crossing in GER days. (C.Cock)

70.   This shows the level crossing at Duck Lees Lane just north of Ponders End in 1958. The original hut has been extended to house the gate wheels. The gates here, unusually, opened across the road, not the railway. (D.Fairhurst)

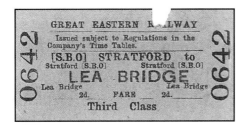

BRIMSDOWN

XI.   The GER opened the station and signal box on the 1st October 1884. Extensive goods facilities surrounded the station, including the short branch to the power station which opened originally in 1907 but was greatly expanded in the mid-1950s when the distinctive cooling towers were added. Coal arrived by rail and barge. A connection also ran for a mile to the Enfield Lock Royal Small Arms factory. Several other rail connected factories surrounded the station. The signal box was extensively damaged by a bomb in 1944 and had to be rebuilt. In LNER days the station was sometimes referred to as Brimsdown for Enfield Highway. During electrification work in the late 1960s, the footbridge was replaced with a subway. The map is from 1911.

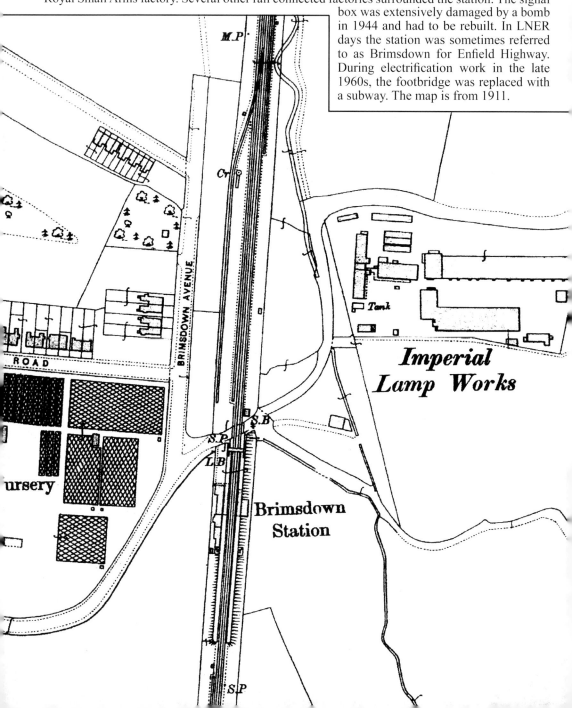

71.   A Liverpool Street bound service calls at the station on 30th November 1957, hauled by N7 class 0-6-2T no. 69710. The scene is quite unspoilt, with the original architecture and canopies, supplemented by an abundance of BR dark blue enamel signs, giving a wonderful atmosphere. (B.Pask)

72.   An express from Cambridge hauled by LNER B2 4-6-0 no. 61644 *Earlham Hall* rattles the windows in Brimsdown signal box as it storms past on its way to Liverpool Street on the 30th November 1957. The goods yard pilot is one of Stratford's J19 class 0-6-0s. This signal box, along with Cheshunt, outlived all the other mechanical boxes on this section and did not finally succumb until August 2002, when Liverpool Street IECC took over the monitoring and control of the level crossing. The box was later demolished. (B.Pask)

73.   On the same day our photographer captures the power, speed and magnificence of BR Standard Pacific 4-6-2 "Britannia" class no. 70041 *Sir John Moore* on an express as we look towards London. The connection to the goods yard can clearly be seen. Ruberoids Ltd still received coal by rail here until 1973. The coal was used to fire the boilers which generated steam for melting bitumen in the manufacturing of roofing felt. (B.Pask)

74.   Just north of Brimsdown in 1959 we see a Stratford based class 16 North British Bo-Bo no. D8403 heading north on the down road with the power station chimneys dominating the background. Coal trains to the power station ended in 1971. These ill-fated locomotives had a very short life after being introduced in 1958; they had numerous engine problems and they had all been withdrawn by 1968. (D.Fairhurst)

75. Cravens class 105 DMU formed of E50360 (leading) and E56420 stands at Brimsdown with a special working due to the overhead power being isolated in July 1977. Note the red flag and detonator just in front of the unit. For many years, the station master's house was home to one of Stratford's drivers and the building survives. (N.L.Cadge)

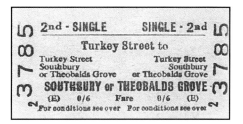

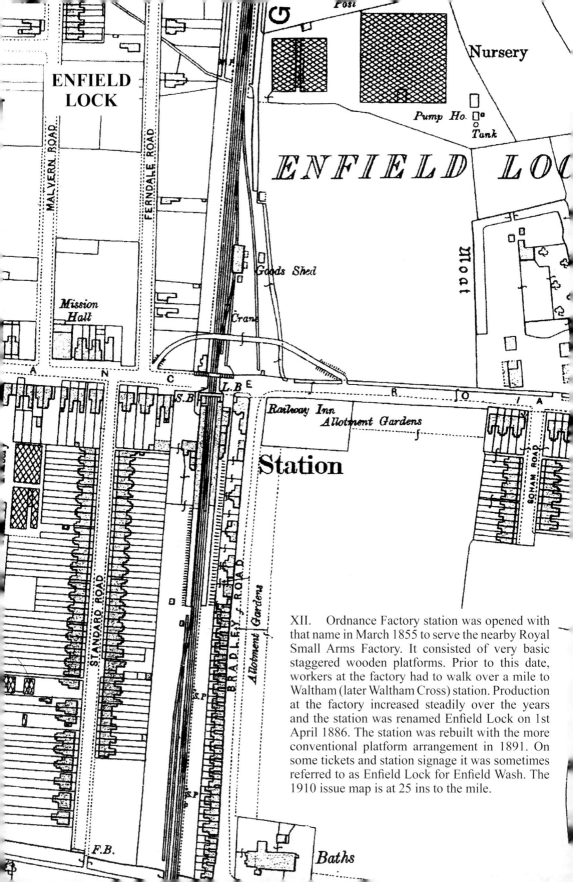

ENFIELD
LOCK

Nursery

Post

Pump Ho.
Tank

ENFIELD LOC

Moat

MALVERN ROAD.

FERNDALE ROAD.

Goods Shed

Crane

Mission
Hall

A   N   C   L.B   E   R   O   A

S.B

Railway Inn
Allotment Gardens

SOHAM ROAD

Station

STANDARD ROAD

BRADLEY ROAD.

Allotment Gardens

S.P

S.P

F.B.

Baths

XII. Ordnance Factory station was opened with that name in March 1855 to serve the nearby Royal Small Arms Factory. It consisted of very basic staggered wooden platforms. Prior to this date, workers at the factory had to walk over a mile to Waltham (later Waltham Cross) station. Production at the factory increased steadily over the years and the station was renamed Enfield Lock on 1st April 1886. The station was rebuilt with the more conventional platform arrangement in 1891. On some tickets and station signage it was sometimes referred to as Enfield Lock for Enfield Wash. The 1910 issue map is at 25 ins to the mile.

76. A rather rustic looking goods yard, complete with vintage wagons and road vehicles, is as it appeared in 1955. The yard was closed in December 1964 as part of the freight rationalisation programme. (D.Fairhurst)

77. The simple, functional and inviting station entrance on the Up side is seen in 1967. This has far more character than many of the modern concrete, glass and steel buildings we are currently greeted by. The Vauxhall Cresta PA, built from 1957 to 1962, would be highly prized by any classic car enthusiast. This exact vehicle appears in another view in this book outside Ponders End station, so it could have belonged to a member of staff. (J.E.Connor coll.)

78.   Looking north, we see the station as it appeared in September 1967. The deep canopy casts a shadow over the extensive station buildings. Behind the doors could be found the station master, porters and a waiting room; luxuries forgotten about by train operators today. (J.E.Connor coll.)

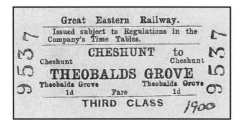

79.   B17 class 4-6-0 no. 61623 *Lambton Castle* is seen on the 12.43 Ely to Liverpool Street express passing the station in 1956. This was a regular working for a Cambridge engine; the loco returned on the 16.36 Liverpool St - Bury St Edmunds. (C.Cock)

80.   Taken from the footbridge which was located just to the south of Enfield Lock, we see a class 125 Derby built 3-car DMU on a Cheshunt to Stratford service in 1959. The livery carried is just as the units were delivered the previous year with the characteristic 'speed whiskers'. The closest track is the siding into the Co-op coal siding. The home signal is 'off' for the up main line, whilst the junction signal is for the up relief line which ran all the way to Brimsdown. (D.Fairhurst)

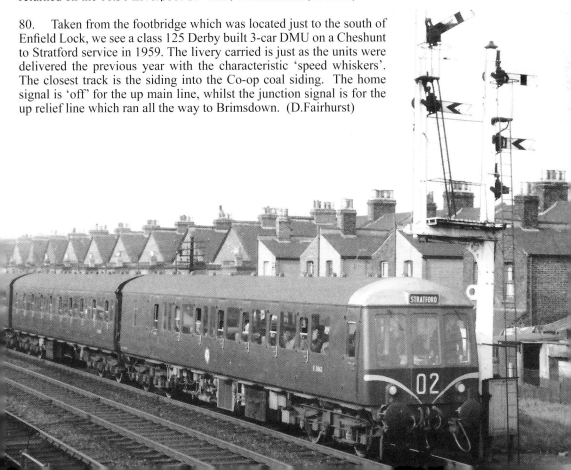

81.　　North British Type 1 class 16 Bo-Bo no. D8401 eases a pick-up freight from the up yard onto the main line over the level crossing in the summer of 1961. The wagons were mainly full of scrap from Jones' yard near Waltham Cross. It was quite common for passenger services to be delayed by shunting at the scrap yard, as wagons had to be hauled onto the up main line, before being propelled back into the yard. (C.Cock)

82.　　The Stratford to Cheshunt line was left out of the 1960 Northeast London electrification scheme, with the consequence that empty stock movements of EMUs between Bishop's Stortford or Hertford East and Ilford Car Sheds had to be loco-hauled over the non-electrified Lea Valley. The only electrified through-route required running via the Southbury Loop and reversal at Liverpool Street, but paths were often not available for this. Here class L1 2-6-4-T no. 67729 is seen approaching Enfield Lock on the down line in September 1960 with a seven-car EMU made up of 4-car no. 508 coupled to a 3-car unit. The stock was being moved to Bishop's Stortford for driver training in preparation for the official opening of electric services in November 1960. (C.Cock)

83.   A most unusual if not unique arrangement of footbridges existed at Enfield Lock, where no less than two footbridges and one perambulator bridge all ran parallel within a stone's throw of each other. All three were demolished in 1968 for the overhead wire clearance and replaced by a subway and a concrete footbridge linking the platforms. This view is taken just prior to the electrification where the goods yard and its connections have been removed, but the old goods shed is still clinging to life. (D.Fairhurst)

84.   The locals became used to the delays at the level crossing. The gentleman on the pushbike is happy to wait instead of carrying his bike over one of the footbridges, whilst the driver of the Vauxhall Victor Estate has no choice. Enfield Lock signal box, blackened by years of grime and brake dust is lurking beside the footbridge on the down platform in this view looking west in 1967. (D.Fairhurst)

85.   Taken just after the electrification in 1969, we are looking at the original GER box dating from 1882. It was a Type 2 McKenzie & Holland design, laterly with a 30 lever frame. It was reduced to the status of a gate box in 1969 and its duties were taken over by CCTV controlled from Brimsdown in 1987. It was demolished without ceremony shortly afterwards. Note that all three bridges have been removed. The new footbridge is behind the photographer. (J.E.Connor coll.)

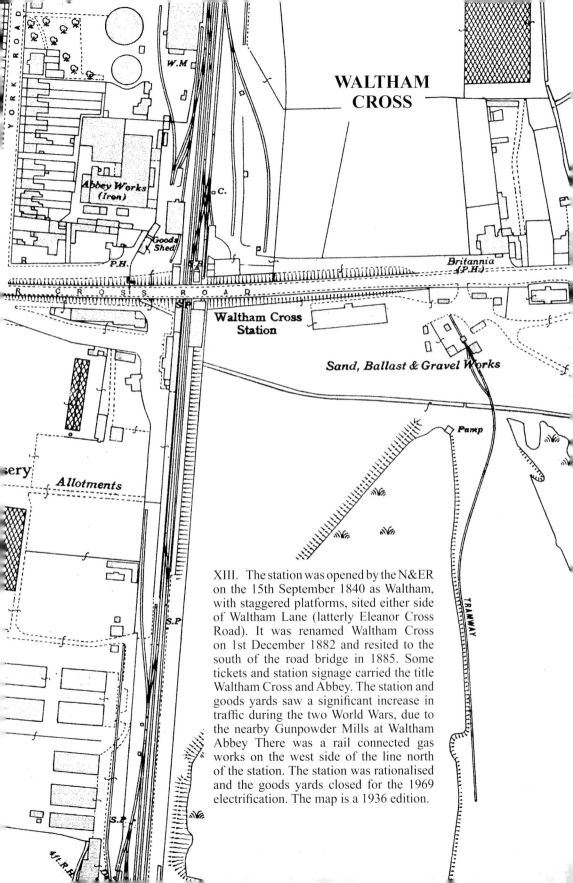

YORK ROAD

W.M

WALTHAM
CROSS

Abbey Works
(Iron)

.C.

Goods
Shed

P.H.

Britannia
(P.H.)

CROSS ROAD

S.P

Waltham Cross
Station

Sand, Ballast & Gravel Works

Pump

:ery

Allotments

S.P

S.P

TRAMWAY

XIII. The station was opened by the N&ER
on the 15th September 1840 as Waltham,
with staggered platforms, sited either side
of Waltham Lane (latterly Eleanor Cross
Road). It was renamed Waltham Cross
on 1st December 1882 and resited to the
south of the road bridge in 1885. Some
tickets and station signage carried the title
Waltham Cross and Abbey. The station and
goods yards saw a significant increase in
traffic during the two World Wars, due to
the nearby Gunpowder Mills at Waltham
Abbey There was a rail connected gas
works on the west side of the line north
of the station. The station was rationalised
and the goods yards closed for the 1969
electrification. The map is a 1936 edition.

4ft R.H.

86.   LNER B1 class 4-6-0 no. 61301, a long-time Cambridge engine, forges a path through the middle of the busy goods yards, as it races towards Liverpool Street with an express from Cambridge on 30th November 1957. The original 1840 down platform would have been on the left before the station was resited south of the road bridge. (B.Pask)

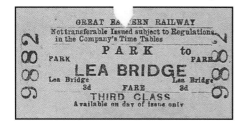

87.   Small wonder that so many of us mourn the passing of the individuality of freight stock and the mixed traffic goods trains. This view of the goods yard looking north in 1959 is packed with various wagons, as numerous staff are loading and unloading them. J19 class 0-6-0 no. 64657, a long serving Stratford engine, rests during shunting whilst working a local goods. A stopping service to Liverpool Street hauled by an L1 class 2-6-4T is approaching the station. (D.Fairhurst)

88.   The long-lost world of goods facilities was recorded on 30th November 1957. The old grounded coach body, which would have undoubtedly served as a comfortable mess room for the yard staff, started off in life as a Great Northern Railway Lavatory Brake 3rd vehicle in 1907. An old L&NER cast iron sign warns that *Trespassers Will Be Prosecuted.* (B.Pask)

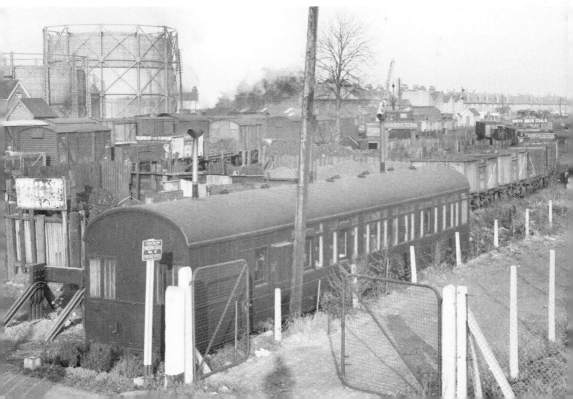

89.   A delightful pre-electrification study is of the signal box looking south in 1967. The 36 lever box dated from 1881 and it survived until 13th January 1969, when new signals and overhead wires brought about its abolition; its duties being absorbed into the Brimsdown panel. In its final years, the box was located under the widened Eleanor Cross Road. (BR/J.E.Connor coll.)

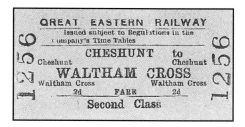

90.   We are looking down side on the 15th October 1967. The atmosphere of a bygone era can be soaked up still. With electrification looming, the Lea Valley line was soon to become modernised with the inevitable unsightly station buildings and bus shelter type waiting rooms that seemed to become the norm. Whilst the connections to the up and down goods yards just beyond the bridge have been severed, the signal box was still in use. (D.Fairhurst)

91.   With the station some distance in the background, we see class 16 North British Bo-Bo no. D8407 with full yellow ends on the up line, with a Harlow Mill to Temple Mills empty limestone hopper train on 15th October 1967. Despite their short career, these locomotives were certainly kept very busy. They had a somewhat untidy but robust appearance when compared to the cleaner lines of the BTH class 15 locomotives. (D.Fairhurst)

CHESHUNT

XIV.   There was no station here when the line opened to Broxbourne in 1840, but the N&ER relented to local pressure by providing a very basic wooden halt known as Cadmore Lane in April 1842. This was used by so few passengers that it closed on 1st June 1842. There were very few people living near the railway at this time and just isolated settlements did not warrant a station. When the ECR took over, they submitted to local pressure and provided a new station at Cheshunt which opened on 31st May 1846. The station was sited further south than Cadmore Lane, at Windmill Lane level crossing.   As with several stations on the line, the wooden platforms were staggered either side of the crossing. The GER built a larger four platform station in 1891 to cope with the additional traffic brought about by the opening of the Churchbury Loop in that year. A large goods yard developed on the west side of the line to handle mainly horticultural, fruit and vegetable traffic generated by the hundreds of glasshouses that bordered the line. The 1914 extract is scaled at 20 ins to the mile.

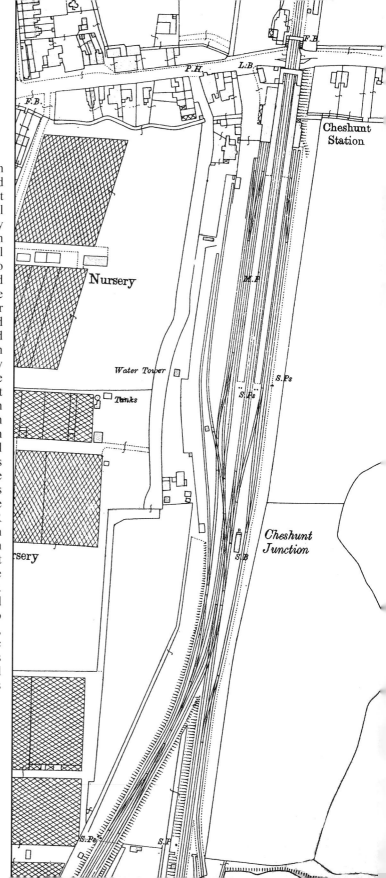

92.   A pleasing view of the 1891 station buildings on the down side as they appeared in the Victorian era viewed from the entrance in Windmill Lane. Added charm is provided by horse-drawn vehicles. (P.Laming coll.)

93.   Seen in the bay platform prior to working a Churchbury Loop line train to Lower Edmonton, is a GER Class Y65, later F7 2-4-2T with a GER two-coach auto train in about 1916. The first carriage was GER no. 633 a clerestory corridor composite built in 1904 and modified for auto-train use. The second carriage was no 522 a clerestory third class built 1906 and also converted, becoming a driving compartment third. In LNER days they were renumbered 63521 and 61328. (P.Laming coll.)

94.   We are looking north in 1958. This was a busy station for passengers and equally so in the goods yard, which survived until 1966 for a daily freight from Temple Mills. There was still a run round facility here in the 1970s for the daily freight which served Jones scrap yard. Old dark blue enamel BR totem signs sit under the LNER 'mint imperial' lamps. (B.Pask)

95.   This rather delightful ex-NER coach had been built at York in 1907 and numbered 809; it was renumbered 2809 by the LNER in 1925. After 1938 it was put into departmental use and given the number E 320530 and is seen here in the bay platform during 1957, when it was being used by the Signal & Telegraph Department as a Staff & Tool Van during preparatory work on the Southbury line electrification. Note the rather oversize chimneys protruding from the roof. (B.Pask)

96.   Captured on the 28th December 1960, just five weeks after the new electric service started, we see green liveried class 302 (AM2) no. 255 about to take the Southbury line with a Bishops Stortford to Liverpool Street service. In the bay is the class 125 Lea Valley line DMU with the next Stratford bound service. Note that the up bay is not electrified. (B.Pask)

97.   One of Stratford's class 125 Rolls Royce powered 3-car DMUs leaves the up bay with a Liverpool Street bound service on 28th December 1960. The 64 lever signal box opened with the Southbury Loop in 1891. It survived until 24th May 2003, when Liverpool Street IECC took over operations. (B.Pask)

GREAT EASTERN RAILWAY.
Issued subject to Regulations in the
Company's Time Tables.
WALTHAM CROSS to
Waltham Cross   Waltham Cross
ENFIELD LOCK
Enfield L. [FOR ENFIELD HIGHWAY] Enfield L.
1d   Fare   1d
[96]   Third Class

7859

GREAT EASTERN RAILWAY
Issued subject to Regulations in the
Company's Time Tables.
WALTHAM CROSS to
Waltham Cross   Waltham Cross
ORDNANCE FACTORY
Ordnance Fac   Ordnance Fac
Third Class

6436

98.   We are looking northwards at the station exterior in 1973. Looking at the brickwork, we can see where the awning used to be. This rather attractive building was subsequently demolished to lengthen the bay platform for 8-car working and replaced by a much less pleasing steel and plastic structure. Such is progress! (J.E.Connor)

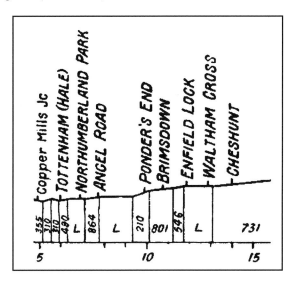

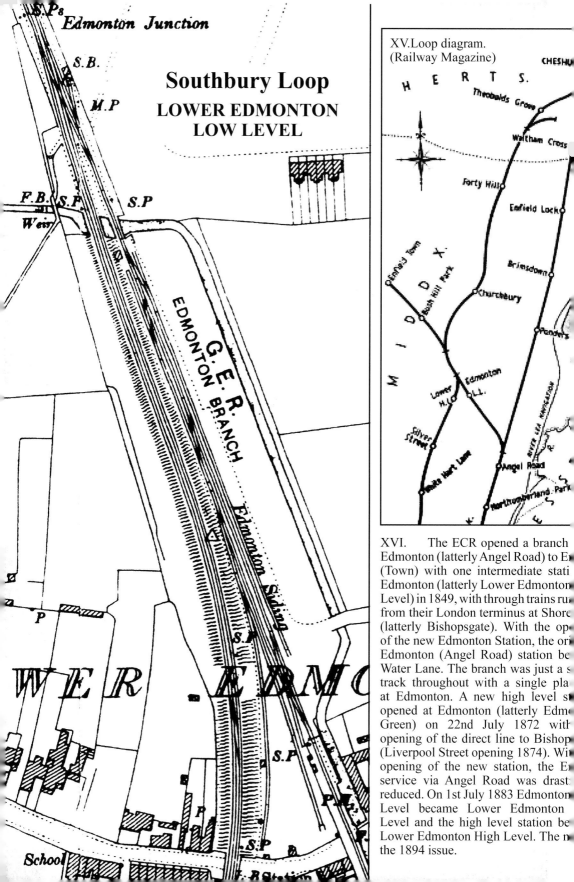

Southbury Loop

LOWER EDMONTON
LOW LEVEL

XV. Loop diagram.
(Railway Magazine)

XVI. The ECR opened a branch
Edmonton (latterly Angel Road) to E
(Town) with one intermediate stati
Edmonton (latterly Lower Edmonton
Level) in 1849, with through trains ru
from their London terminus at Shore
(latterly Bishopsgate). With the op
of the new Edmonton Station, the or
Edmonton (Angel Road) station be
Water Lane. The branch was just a s
track throughout with a single pla
at Edmonton. A new high level s
opened at Edmonton (latterly Edm
Green) on 22nd July 1872 with
opening of the direct line to Bishop
(Liverpool Street opening 1874). Wi
opening of the new station, the E
service via Angel Road was drast
reduced. On 1st July 1883 Edmonton
Level became Lower Edmonton
Level and the high level station be
Lower Edmonton High Level. The n
the 1894 issue.

99.   This very rare and early view of Lower Edmonton Low Level signal box was taken around 1905. The box was opened by the GER in about 1877 and lasted until 1934 when a ground frame, released electronically from Edmonton Junction, took over control of the level crossing gates. (C.Cock coll.)

100.   Although the station officially closed on 11th September 1939, it was occasionally reopened during engineering possessions when Enfield Town services were diverted along the Lea Valley to Angel Road, thence by the original route. Such a diverted service is seen here on 19th October 1958 as a Liverpool Street to Enfield Town service, hauled by N7 class 0-6-2T no. 69671, arrives at the old platform. Beyond the level crossing is an additional platform, built in 1899 for workmen's trains. This reduced the need to have the crossing closed for lengthy periods. (B.Pask)

101.   Leaving Lower Edmonton, N7 class 0-6-2T no. 69668 hauls an impressive 10-coach Enfield Town service formed of two quint-art LNER sets of articulated stock. To the left, surrounded by signal & telegraph engineers can be seen a J15 0-6-0 goods engine waiting to leave the Low Level goods yard with a short freight. The year is 1961 and the overhead wires are installed for the imminent arrival of the first electric trains. (T.Wright)

102.   During the early months of 1963 the Lea Valley line was closed for engineering work and once again the old Angel Road to Lower Edmonton branch was utilised for diverted trains. Here we see a Cheshunt bound class 125 DMU leaving Lower Edmonton Low Level as it heads towards Edmonton Junction and the electrified main line to Enfield Town is seen on the embankment to the left. (D.Fairhurst)

103.   A class 20 English Electric Type 1 Bo-Bo diesel in early green livery with half yellow warning panels has the distinction of working the track-lifting train in 1965. The local children and their parents are obviously excited by the very last train at the old platform and have turned out in force to witness the event. The platform here had a footpath running across it at right angles and steps down to track level which were covered by a steel plate when a train arrived. (D.Fairhurst)

104.   This is Edmonton Junction signal box looking north towards Enfield Town in 1911. The box dated from 1872 and was originally fitted with a 25 lever frame. The Angel Road branch leading to the Low Level station and goods yard is on the right. The footbridge was a favourite haunt for trainspotters and photographers. (GER)

105. Here is some pure GER nostalgia in the shape of Bury Street Junction signal box in 1911. We are looking south towards Lower Edmonton and the road bridge carries Bury Street itself. This was a McKenzie & Holland box of 1893, which was downgraded to a ground frame in 1934 and the base was used as a relay room during for the colour light signalling installation is still in use. The lines on the left head towards Churchbury, where the passenger service had ceased two years previously, and the lines on the right lead to Enfield Town. (GER/A.Rush coll.)

106. On 26th June 1976 an 8-car class 309 Clacton unit worked a Sunday School special from Enfield Town to Clacton. This rare occasion was recorded at Bury Street Junction. The brick base of the former signal box can just about be seen by the rearmost cab. Even class 306 sliding door units built in 1949 were recorded at Enfield Town in the run up to Christmas in the 1970s on postal trains. (N.L.Cadge)

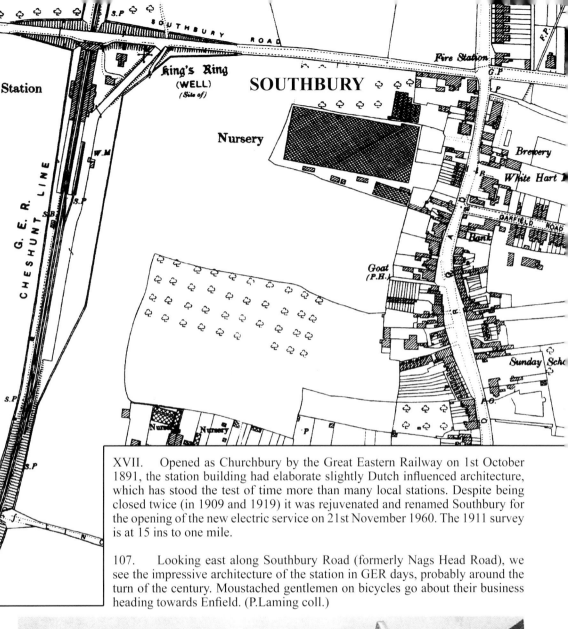

Station

SOUTHBURY

King's Ring
(WELL)
(Site of)

Nursery

Fire Station

Brewery

White Hart

GARFIELD ROAD

Bank

Goat
(P.H.)

Sunday Sch

P.O.

Nursery   Nursery

G. E. R. LINE

CHESHUNT LINE

XVII.   Opened as Churchbury by the Great Eastern Railway on 1st October 1891, the station building had elaborate slightly Dutch influenced architecture, which has stood the test of time more than many local stations. Despite being closed twice (in 1909 and 1919) it was rejuvenated and renamed Southbury for the opening of the new electric service on 21st November 1960. The 1911 survey is at 15 ins to one mile.

107.   Looking east along Southbury Road (formerly Nags Head Road), we see the impressive architecture of the station in GER days, probably around the turn of the century. Moustached gentlemen on bicycles go about their business heading towards Enfield. (P.Laming coll.)

108. On the 15th June 1957, The Railway Enthusiasts Club ran a railtour from Fenchurch Street to Kings Cross using ex-works BR Standard 2-6-4T no 80135 and N2 0-6-2T no. 69594. The train is seen here on the up road at Churchbury during its run from Cheshunt to South Tottenham, where the train reversed and went to Palace Gates. The signal box dated from 1891. A platform extension has been built around the box, which closed on 3rd July 1960, after colour light signals were introduced. (H.B.Oliver)

109. The exterior is seen on the day of reopening, on 21st November 1960. The large poster proclaims "Southbury – Frequent Electric Trains to the City". Extensive renovation work had been carried out in the old 1891 booking hall and ticket office. (B.Pask)

110. Class 305/1 no 433 runs into the station with a Cheshunt bound service in January 1975. The area to the right was formerly the goods yard and has been taken over by a scrap dealer. On a more positive note, the old GER canopies are intact. (N.L.Cadge)

CARTERHATCH LANE HALT

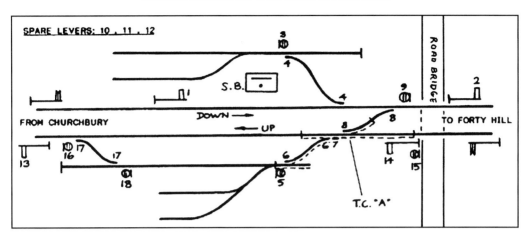

XVIII.   When the line was constructed, it was intended to have a station at Carterhatch Lane, but the population of the area in the early 1890s did not warrant such expenditure and the idea was abandoned. World War I brought about a need for a new halt at the site, formed of a very basic wooden platform with a couple of oil lamps, just long enough for two coaches. Remembering that the up line was used for wagon storage at this time, there was no need for an up platform and push-pull trains in both directions used the down platform. The halt was opened for business on 12th June 1916 and was served by 15 trains each way. It closed seven months after hostilities ended on 1st July 1919. The diagram is from 1958 and shows the temporary sidings laid by the British Insulated Cable Company (BICC) for the Southbury, Hertford East and Bishops Stortford electrification project.

111.   The late 1950s electrification project on the Southbury Loop saw a large open area at Cartherhatch Lane converted into a depot for the overhead line department. Here we see the depot looking north in 1958. Carterhatch Lane temporary signal box is in the middle of the picture. The central roadway provides a storage area for the prefabricated overhead gantries. The former down platform was situated immediately beyond the over bridge. (D.Fairhurst)

112.   Class J39 0-6-0 no. 64775 leaves the depot with a wiring train in 1959. The train conveys a crane for the installation of new gantries. Work on this project started in 1956. This was a Stratford engine and ironically its career ended just over a year later. Very much a case of digging your own grave! (D.Fairhurst)

113.   Although this image is slightly out of focus, it captures a rare moment in time, as a class 125 DMU diverted from the Lea Valley passes the overhead line depot in 1960. The wiring trains are formed of a wonderful collection of antique coaches including some GER vehicles. The signal box was opened early 1958 to control movements in and out of the sidings. It was rarely used after the electrification work finished. It was downgraded to ground frame on 7th July 1960. All the controls were removed in February 1965 and it was closed. (D.Fairhurst)

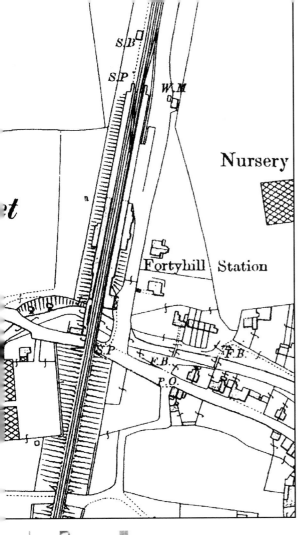

Nursery

Fortyhill Station

TURKEY STREET

XIX.   Forty Hill opened on the 1st October 1891 with the opening of the five mile long Churchbury Loop line. At this time there were only a handful of cottages near the station and Forty Hill village was a mile away to the west. The main Hertford Road was half a mile to the east. Its fortunes were therefore rather poor and passenger numbers on the initial one train per hour were dismal. Unsurprisingly closure came exactly 18 years after opening, in 1909. A brief spell of activity (described earlier) in the World War I saw the station given a second chance, but this ended on 1st July 1919. A small goods yard was provided on the up side of the line north of the station. The station was renamed Turkey Street and reopened on 21st November 1960 when the Loop line was electrified. The map is the 1910 issue.

114.   By good fortune, when the Loop was electrified, there was a decision to refurbish the old station buildings as an economy measure, thereby saving some very historic structures. Here we look north at the up side buildings and ticket office as they appeared on 28th December 1960, just five weeks after the new electric service had started. (B.Pask)

115.   Due to engineering work on the Lea Valley electrification, the 08.36 Liverpool Street to Cambridge service has been diverted via the Southbury Loop and is seen heading north through Turkey Street on 2nd June 1968. It is hauled by class 37 English Electric Type 3 Co-Co no. D6711 in BR green with full yellow ends. (P.Paye)

116.   Class 305/2 (AM5/2) EMU no. 502 leaves the station with a Cheshunt to Liverpool Street bound service in January 1975. Known by railwaymen as slam-door stock, these units were popular with passengers, but less so with the railway management. There were several incidents where passengers standing on platforms were hit by doors being opened too early before the train had come to a stand. (N.L.Cadge)

THEOBALDS GROVE

XX.   The station opened on 1st October 1891. It was a rather expensive station to build due to the need for the busy Hertford Road to be crossed by a bridge rather than a level crossing, thereby entailing large scale embankments to be constructed either side. It suffered the same failures as the other stations on the Loop, but fared slightly better with higher passenger numbers when open in GER days, due to its proximity to local housing. New life was breathed into the old station by the electrification project and it reopened on 21st November 1960. A small goods yard existed here until 1966. The 1936 survey is shown.

117. A delightful Victorian study of the station entrance looking west is from about 1900 during the brief spell of operation by the GER. A bearded gentleman driving a horse and trap with a passenger sporting an even larger beard is a wonderful reminder of the simple life that existed prior to the proliferation of motor cars. Children in their finest outfits are probably heading for Sunday school. (P.Laming collection)

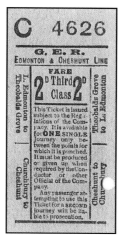

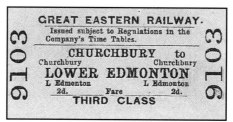

118.   This is a rare early view of a GER Auto-Train, sporting a Cheshunt destination board approaching the station in 1915. It is being propelled by a GER class F7 2-4-2T, which had only been in service for five years. Originally classed as Y65, there were only 12 engines in the class, which were built between 1909 and 1910. The service is one of the short-lived wartime trains provided for munitions workers. (LCGB/K.Nunn coll.)

119.   An immaculate LNER class J17 0-6-0 tender loco no. 8194 with a Belpaire firebox heads north through the station. The driver has resisted the temptation to open the regulator as he passes under a line of washing hung between the canopies by the residents of the station buildings. The line was served by a daily goods train at this time and occasionally diverted trains off the Lea Valley line. The signal box at the London end of the down platform dates from the opening of the line in 1891 and it closed on 3rd July 1960. This photograph was taken during March 1947, when the Lea Valley line was closed due to flooding. (LNER)

120.   A class 302 (AM2) 8-car EMU with no. 273 leading enters the refurbished station on 28th December 1960 with a Liverpool Street service. The novelty of electric passenger trains running over this long-forgotten route brought about many benefits for local business and commuters. The service is just five weeks old and Theobalds Grove gradually became the busiest station on the Loop. Trains from London divided at Broxbourne then went on to Hertford East or Bishops Stortford. (B.Pask)

BISHOP'S STORTFORD, HERTFORD (EAST), BROXBOURNE, SOUTHBURY, TOTTENHAM, STRATFORD and LIVERPOOL STREET

MONDAYS TO FRIDAYS

Miles (cut off)	Miles	Miles			am	am		am	am 2	am	am 2	am 2	am		am 2	am 2	am	am 2	am	am 2	am 2
					Mondays only; From Norwich dep 10 20 pm (Sundays)	Except Mondays; From Norwich dep 10 40 pm															
—	—	—	**BISHOP'S STORTFORD** ..	dep	1 21	1 31	..	4 18	..	5 18	..	..	5 58	..	..	..	6 18	..	6 38	..	..
3½	3½	3½	**Sawbridgeworth**	,,		....	....	4 23	....	5 23	....	....	6 3	....	....	....	6 23	....	6 43	....	....
5¾	5¾	5¾	**Harlow Mill**	,,		..	..	4 27	..	5 27	..	..	6 7	..	..	..	6 27	..	6 47	..	..
7½	7½	7½	**Harlow Town**	,,		1 43	....	4 31	....	5 31	....	....	6 11	....	....	....	6 31	....	6 51	....	....
0¼	10¼	10¼	**Roydon**	,,		..	..	4 35	..	5 35	..	..	6 15	..	..	..	6 35	..	6 55	..	..
3¼	13¼	13¼	**Broxbourne & Hoddesdon** ..	arr		....	....	4 40	....	5 40	....	....	6 20	....	....	....	6 40	....	7 0	....	....
—	—	—	**HERTFORD (East)** ..	dep			..	4 23	..	5 23	..	..	6 3	..	..	..	6 23	..	6 43	..	..
2	—	—	**Ware**	,,			....	4 27	....	5 27	....	....	6 7	....	....	....	6 27	....	6 47	....	....
4	—	—	**St. Margaret's**	,,			..	4 30	..	5 30	..	..	6 10	..	..	..	6 30	..	6 50	..	..
5¼	—	—	**Rye House**	,,			....	4 33	....	5 33	....	....	6 13	....	....	....	6 33	....	6 53	....	....
7¼	—	—	**Broxbourne & Hoddesdon**	arr			..	4 38	..	5 38	..	..	6 18	..	..	..	6 38	..	6 58	..	..
—	—	—	**Broxbourne & Hoddesdon** ..	dep			....	4 42	....	5 42	....	6 15	6 22	....	....	6 35	6 42	6 55	7 2	....	7 13
6¼	16¼	16¼	**Cheshunt** ..	,,			..	4 47	4 54	5 47	5 54	6 20	6 27	..	6 34	6 40	6 47	7 0	7 7	7 14	7 18
7¼	—	—	**Theobalds Grove**	,,			....	4 50	....	5 50	....	....	6 30	....	....	....	6 50	....	7 10	....	....
8½	—	—	**Turkey Street**	,,			..	4 53	..	5 53	..	..	6 33	..	..	..	6 53	..	7 13	..	..
0¼	—	—	**Southbury**	,,			....	4 56	....	5 56	....	....	6 36	....	....	....	6 56	....	7 16	....	....
2	—	—	**Lower Edmonton**	,,			..	5 0	..	6 0	..	..	6 40	..	..	..	7 0	..	7 20	..	..
—	17½	17½	**Waltham Cross and Abbey** ..	,,	1 43		....	....	4 56	....	5 56	6 22	....	....	6 36	6 42	....	7 2	....	7 16	7 20
—	18½	18½	**Enfield Lock**	,,	..		..	..	4 59	..	5 59	6 25	..	..	6 39	6 45	..	7 5	..	7 19	7 23
—	19½	19½	**Brimsdown**	,,	....		....	....	5 1	....	6 1	6 27	....	....	6 41	6 47	....	7 7	....	7 21	7 25
—	20½	20½	**Ponders End**	,,	..		..	..	5 4	..	6 4	6 30	..	..	6 44	6 50	..	7 10	..	7 24	7 28
—	22½	22½	**Angel Road**	,,	....		....	....	5 8	....	6 8	6 34	....	....	6 48	6 54	....	7 14	....	7 28	7 32
—	23¼	23¼	**Northumberland Park**	,,	..		..	..	5 10	..	6 10	6 36	..	..	6 50	6 56	..	7 16	..	7 30	7 34
—	24¼	24¼	**Tottenham**	,,	1 57		....	....	5 12	....	6 12	6 38	....	....	6 52	6 58	....	7 18	....	7 32	7 36
—	—	26¼	**Lea Bridge**	,,	..	..	..	..	5 15	..	6 15	..	..	..	6 55	..	..	..	..	7 35	..
—	—	28½	**STRATFORD**	arr	2 7	2 8	....	....	5 22	....	6 22	....	....	....	7 2	....	....	....	....	7 42	....
—	26¼	—	**Clapton** ..	dep	..	..	..	..	..	..	..	6 42	..	..	..	7 2	..	7 22	..	..	7 40
—	27½	—	**Hackney Downs**	,,	....	....	....	....	....	....	....	....	....	....	....	....	....	....	....	....	....
0¾	30¼	—	**LIVERPOOL STREET** ..	arr	2 20	2 20	..	5 16	..	6 16	..	6 51	6 56	..	..	7 11	7 16	7 31	7 36	..	7 49

MONDAYS TO FRIDAYS—*continued*

		am	am 2	am	am 2	am 2	am 2	am	am 2	am	am 2	am	am 2	am	am 2	am	am	am 2	am 2	am	am	am 2
						To North Woolwich arr 8 35 am				From Cambridge dep 7 0 am			From Audley End dep 7 48 am	Miniature Buffet Car; From Cambridge dep 7 40 am			From Ely dep 7 25 am				Miniature Buffet Car; From Cambridge dep 8 0 am	
ISHOP'S STORTFORD ..	dep	6 58	..	7 18	7 30		..	7 38	7 50	7 55	..	7 58	8 10	8 15	..	8 18	8 35	..	..	8 38	8 55	..
awbridgeworth	,,	7 3	....	7 23	....		....	7 43	....	....	....	8 3	....	....	....	8 23	....	....	....	8 43	....	....
arlow Mill	,,	7 7	..	7 27	..		..	7 47	..	..	..	8 7	..	..	..	8 27	..	..	..	8 47	..	..
arlow Town	,,	7 11	....	7 31	7 40		....	7 51	8 0	....	....	8 11	8 20	....	....	8 31	....	....	....	8 51	....	....
oydon	,,	7 15	..	7 35	..		..	7 55	..	..	..	8 15	..	..	..	8 35	..	..	..	8 55	..	..
roxbourne & Hoddesdon ..	arr	7 20	....	7 40	....		....	8 0	....	....	....	8 20	....	....	....	8 40	....	....	....	9 0	....	....
HERTFORD (East) ..	dep	7 3	..	7 23	..		..	7 43	..		..	8 3			..	8 23		..	..	8 43		..
Ware	,,	7 7	....	7 27	....		....	7 47	....		....	8 7			....	8 27		....	....	8 47		....
St. Margaret's	,,	7 10	..	7 30	..		..	7 50	..		..	8 10			..	8 30		..	..	8 50		..
Rye House	,,	7 13	....	7 33	....		....	7 53	....		....	8 13			....	8 33		....	....	8 53		....
Broxbourne & Hoddesdon	arr	7 18	..	7 38	..		..	7 58	..		..	8 18			..	8 38		..	..	8 58		..
roxbourne & Hoddesdon ..	dep	7 22	7 33	7 42	....	....	7 53	8 2	....		8 13	8 22			8 33	8 42		....	8 53	9 2		9 13
heshunt ..	,,	7 27	7 38	7 47	..	7 54	7 58	8 7	..		8 18	8 27			8 38	8 47		..	8 58	9 7		9 18
Theobalds Grove	,,	7 30	....	7 50	....			8 10	....		....	8 30			....	8 50		....	....	9 10		....
Turkey Street	,,	7 33	..	7 53	..	..	..	8 13	..		..	8 33			..	8 53		..	..	9 13		..
Southbury	,,	7 36	....	7 56	....			8 16	....		....	8 36			....	8 56		....	....	9 16		....
Lower Edmonton	,,	7 40	..	8 0	..			8 20	..		..	8 40			..	9 0		..	..	9 20		..
altham Cross and Abbey ..	,,	....	7 40	....	....	7 56	8 0	....	....	....	8 20	....	....		8 40	....	....	....	9 0	....		9 20
nfield Lock	,,	..	7 43	..	..	7 59	8 3	..	..	..	8 23	..	..		8 43	..	..	..	9 3	..		9 23
rimsdown	,,	....	7 45	....	....	8 1	8 5	....	....	....	8 25	....	....		8 45	....	....	9 1	9 5	....		9 25
onders End	,,	..	7 48	..	..	8 4	8 8	..	..	..	8 28	..	..		8 48	..	..	9 4	9 8	..		9 28
ngel Road	,,	....	7 52	....	....	8 8	8 12	....	....	....	8 32	....	....		8 52	....	....	9 8	9 12	....		9 32
orthumberland Park	,,	..	7 54	..	..	8 10	8 14	..	..	..	8 34	..	..		8 54	..	..	9 10	9 14	..		9 34
ottenham	,,	....	7 56	....	....	8 12	8 16	....	....	....	8 36	....	....		8 56	....	....	9 12	9 16	....		9 36
Lea Bridge ..	,,	..	..	..	..	8 15	..	..	..	..	..	..	..	..	..	..	..	9 15	..	..	..	..
STRATFORD	arr	....	....	....	....	8L22	....	....	....	....	....	....	....	....	....	....	....	9 22	....	....	....	....
lapton ..	dep	..	8 0	..	..	..	8 20	..	..	..	8 40	..	..	..	9 0	..	..	..	9 20	..	..	9 40
ackney Downs	,,	....	....	....	....	....	....	....	....	....	....	....	....	....	....	....	....	....	....	....	....	....
IVERPOOL STREET ..	arr	7 56	8 9	8 16	8 12	..	8 29	8 36	8 32	8 38	8 50	8 56	8 52	8 58	9 10	9 16	9 18	..	9 29	9 36	9 38	9 49

2 Second class only.   L Stratford (Low Level)

Peak hour service for the return journey back into London in the Summer of 1963.

Middleton Press

EVOLVING THE ULTIMATE RAIL ENCYCLOPEDIA

Easebourne Lane, Midhurst, West Sussex. GU29 9AZ   Tel:01730 813169

www.middletonpress.co.uk   email:info@middletonpress.co.uk
A-978 0 906520   B- 978 1 873793   C- 978 1 901706   D-978 1 904474
E - 978 1 906008   F - 978 1 908174

All titles listed below were in print at time of publication - please check current availability by looking at our website - *www.middletonpress.co.uk* or by requesting a Brochure which includes our *LATEST* RAILWAY TITLES also our TRAMWAY, TROLLEYBUS, MILITARY and COASTAL series

A

Abergavenny to Merthyr C 91 8
Abertillery & Ebbw Vale Lines D 84 5
Aberystwyth to Carmarthen E 90 1
Allhallows - Branch Line to A 62 8
Alton - Branch Lines to A 11 6
Andover to Southampton A 82 6
Ascot - Branch Lines around A 64 2
Ashburton - Branch Line to B 95 4
Ashford - Steam to Eurostar B 67 1
Ashford to Dover A 48 2
Austrian Narrow Gauge D 04 3
Avonmouth - BL around D 42 5
Aylesbury to Rugby D 91 3

B

Baker Street to Uxbridge D 90 6
Bala to Llandudno E 87 1
Banbury to Birmingham D 27 2
Banbury to Cheltenham E 63 5
Bangor to Holyhead F 01 7
Bangor to Portmadoc E 72 7
Barking to Southend C 80 2
Barmouth to Pwllheli E 53 6
Barry - Branch Lines around D 50 0
Bartlow - Branch Lines to F 27 7
Bath Green Park to Bristol C 36 9
Bath to Evercreech Junction A 60 4
Beamish 40 years on rails E94 9
Bedford to Wellingborough D 31 9
Birmingham to Wolverhampton E253
Bletchley to Cambridge D 94 4
Bletchley to Rugby E 07 9
Bodmin - Branch Lines around B 83 1
Bournemouth to Evercreech Jn A 46 8
Bournemouth to Weymouth A 57 4
Bradshaw's Guide 1866 F 05 5
Bradshaw's History F18 5
Bradshaw's Rail Times 1850 F 13 0
Bradshaw's Rail Times 1895 F 11 6
Branch Lines series - see town names
Brecon to Neath D 43 2
Brecon to Newport D 16 6
Brecon to Newtown E 06 2
Brighton to Eastbourne A 16 1
Brighton to Worthing A 03 1
Bristol to Taunton D 03 6
Bromley South to Rochester B 23 7
Bromsgrove to Birmingham D 87 6
Bromsgrove to Gloucester D 73 9
Broxbourne to Cambridge F16 1
Brunel - A railtour D 74 6
Bude - Branch Line to B 29 9
Burnham to Evercreech Jn B 68 0

C

Cambridge to Ely D 55 5
Canterbury - BLs around B 58 9
Cardiff to Dowlais (Cae Harris) F 47 5
Cardiff to Pontypridd E 95 6
Cardiff to Swansea E 42 0
Carlisle to Hawick E 85 7
Carmarthen to Fishguard E 66 6
Caterham & Tattenham Corner B251
Central & Southern Spain NG E 91 8
Chard and Yeovil - BLs a C 30 7
Charing Cross to Dartford A 75 8
Charing Cross to Orpington A 96 3
Cheddar - Branch Line to B 90 9
Cheltenham to Andover C 43 7
Cheltenham to Redditch D 81 4
Chester Northgate to Manchester F 51
Chester to Birkenhead F 21 5
Chester to Rhyl E 93 2
Chester to Warrington F 40 6
Chichester to Portsmouth A 14 7
Clacton and Walton - BLs to F 04 8
Clapham Jn to Beckenham Jn B 36 7

Cleobury Mortimer - BLs a E 18 5
Clevedon & Portishead - BLs to D180
Consett to South Shields E 57 4
Cornwall Narrow Gauge D 56 2
Corris and Vale of Rheidol E 65 9
Craven Arms to Llandeilo E 35 2
Craven Arms to Wellington E 33 8
Crawley to Littlehampton A 34 5
Cromer - Branch Lines around C 26 0
Croydon to East Grinstead B 48 0
Crystal Palace & Catford Loop B 87 1
Cyprus Narrow Gauge E 13 0

D

Darjeeling Revisited F 09 3
Darlington Leamside Newcastle E 28 4
Darlington to Newcastle D 98 2
Dartford to Sittingbourne B 34 3
Denbigh - Branch Lines around F 32 1
Derwent Valley - BL to the D 06 7
Devon Narrow Gauge E 09 3
Didcot to Banbury D 02 9
Didcot to Swindon C 84 0
Didcot to Winchester C 13 0
Dorset & Somerset NG D 76 0
Douglas - Laxey - Ramsey E 75 8
Douglas to Peel C 88 8
Douglas to Port Erin C 55 0
Douglas to Ramsey D 39 5
Dover to Ramsgate A 78 9
Dublin Northwards in 1950s E 31 4
Dunstable - Branch Lines to E 27 7

E

Ealing to Slough C 42 0
Eastbourne to Hastings A 27 7
East Cornwall Mineral Railways D 22 7
East Croydon to Three Bridges A 53 6
Eastern Spain Narrow Gauge E 56 7
East Grinstead - BLs to A 07 9
East London - Branch Lines of C 44 4
East London Line B 80 0
East of Norwich - Branch Lines E 69 7
Effingham Junction - BLs a A 74 1
Ely to Norwich C 90 1
Enfield Town & Palace Gates D 32 6
Epsom to Horsham A 30 7
Eritrean Narrow Gauge E 38 3
Euston to Harrow & Wealdstone C 89 5
Exeter to Barnstaple B 15 2
Exeter to Newton Abbot C 49 9
Exeter to Tavistock B 69 5
Exmouth - Branch Lines to B 00 8

F

Fairford - Branch Line to A 52 9
Falmouth, Helston & St. Ives C 74 1
Fareham to Salisbury A 67 3
Faversham to Dover B 05 3
Felixstowe & Aldeburgh - BL to D 20 3
Fenchurch Street to Barking C 20 8
Festiniog - 50 yrs of enterprise C 83 3
Festiniog 1946-55 E 01 7
Festiniog in the Fifties B 68 8
Festiniog in the Sixties B 91 6
Ffestiniog in Colour 1955-82 F 25 3
Finsbury Park to Alexandra Pal C 02 8
Frome to Bristol B 77 0

G

Galashiels to Edinburgh F 52 9
Gloucester to Bristol D 35 7
Gloucester to Cardiff D 66 1
Gosport - Branch Lines around A 36 9
Greece Narrow Gauge D 72 2

H

Hampshire Narrow Gauge D 36 4
Harrow to Watford D 14 2
Harwich & Hadleigh - BLs to F 02 4

Hastings to Ashford A 37 6
Hawick to Galashiels F 36 9
Hawkhurst - Branch Line to A 66 6
Hayling - Branch Line to A 12 3
Hay-on-Wye - BL around D 92 0
Haywards Heath to Seaford A 28 4
Hemel Hempstead - BLs to D 88 3
Henley, Windsor & Marlow - BLa C77 2
Hereford to Newport D 54 8
Hertford & Hatfield - BLs a E 58 1
Hertford Loop E 71 0
Hexham to Carlisle D 75 3
Hexham to Hawick F 08 6
Hitchin to Peterborough D 07 4
Holborn Viaduct to Lewisham A 81 9
Horsham - Branch Lines to A 02 4
Huntingdon - Branch Line to A 93 2

I

Ilford to Shenfield C 97 0
Ilfracombe - Branch Line to B 21 3
Industrial Rlys of the South East A 09 3
Ipswich to Saxmundham C 41 3
Isle of Wight Lines - 50 yrs C 12 3
Italy Narrow Gauge F 17 8

K

Kent Narrow Gauge C 45 1
Kidderminster to Shrewsbury E 10 9
Kingsbridge - Branch Line to C 98 7
Kings Cross to Potters Bar E 62 8
Kingston & Hounslow Loops A 83 3
Kingswear - Branch Line to C 17 8

L

Lambourn - Branch Line to C 70 3
Launceston & Princetown - BLs C 19 2
Lewisham to Dartford A 92 5
Lines around Wimbledon B 75 6
Liverpool Street to Chingford D 01 2
Liverpool Street to Ilford C 34 5
Llandeilo to Swansea E 46 8
London Bridge to Addiscombe B 20 6
London Bridge to East Croydon A 58 1
Longmoor - Branch Lines to A 41 3
Looe - Branch Line to C 22 2
Lowestoft - BLs around E 40 6
Ludlow to Hereford E 14 7
Lydney - Branch Lines around E 26 0
Lyme Regis - Branch Line to A 45 1
Lynton - Branch Line to B 04 6

M

Machynlleth to Barmouth E 54 3
Maesteg and Tondu Lines E 06 2
Majorca & Corsica Narrow Gauge F 41 3
March - Branch Lines around B 09 1
Marylebone to Rickmansworth D 49 4
Melton Constable to Yarmouth Bch E031
Midhurst - Branch Lines of E 78 9
Midhurst - Branch Lines to F 00 0
Minehead - Branch Line to A 80 2
Mitcham Junction Lines B 01 5
Mitchell & company C 59 8
Monmouth - Branch Lines to E 20 8
Monmouthshire Eastern Valleys D 71 5
Moretonhampstead - BL to C 27 7
Moreton-in-Marsh to Worcester D 26 5
Mountain Ash to Neath D 80 7

N

Newbury to Westbury C 66 6
Newcastle to Hexham D 69 2
Newport (IOW) - Branch Lines to A 26 0
Newquay - Branch lines to C 71 0
Newton Abbot to Plymouth C 60 4
Newtown to Aberystwyth E 41 3
North East German NG D 44 9
Northern Alpine Narrow Gauge F 37 6
Northern France Narrow Gauge C 75 8

Northern Spain Narrow Gauge E 83 3
North London Line B 94 7
North of Birmingham F 55 0
North Woolwich - BLs around C 65 9
Nottingham to Lincoln F 43 7

O

Ongar - Branch Line to E 05 5
Orpington to Tonbridge B 03 9
Oswestry - Branch Lines around E 60 4
Oswestry to Whitchurch E 81 9
Oxford to Bletchley D 57 9
Oxford to Moreton-in-Marsh D 15 9

P

Paddington to Ealing C 37 6
Paddington to Princes Risborough C819
Padstow - Branch Line to B 54 1
Pembroke and Cardigan - BLs to F 29 1
Peterborough to Kings Lynn E 32 1
Plymouth - BLs around B 98 5
Plymouth to St. Austell C 63 5
Pontypool to Mountain Ash D 65 4
Pontypridd to Merthyr F 14 7
Pontypridd to Port Talbot E 86 4
Porthmadog 1954-94 - BLa B 31 2
Portmadoc 1923-46 - BLa B 13 8
Portsmouth to Southampton A 31 4
Portugal Narrow Gauge E 67 3
Potters Bar to Cambridge D 70 8
Princes Risborough - BL to D 05 0
Princes Risborough to Banbury C 85 7

R

Reading to Basingstoke B 27 5
Reading to Didcot C 79 6
Reading to Guildford A 47 5
Redhill to Ashford A 73 4
Return to Blaenau 1970-82 C 64 2
Rhyl to Bangor F 15 4
Rhymney & New Tredegar Lines E 48 2
Rickmansworth to Aylesbury D 61 6
Romania & Bulgaria NG E 23 9
Romneyrail C 32 1
Ross-on-Wye - BLs around E 30 7
Ruabon to Barmouth E 84 0
Rugby to Birmingham E 37 6
Rugby to Loughborough F 12 3
Rugby to Stafford F 07 9
Ryde to Ventnor A 19 2

S

Salisbury to Westbury B 39 8
Sardinia and Sicily Narrow Gauge F 50 5
Saxmundham to Yarmouth C 69 7
Saxony Narrow Gauge D 47 0
Seaton & Sidmouth - BLs to A 95 6
Selsey - Branch Line to A 04 8
Sheerness - Branch Line to B 16 2
Shenfield to Ipswich E 96 3
Shrewsbury - Branch Line to A 86 4
Shrewsbury to Chester E 70 3
Shrewsbury to Crewe F 48 2
Shrewsbury to Ludlow E 21 5
Shrewsbury to Newtown E 29 1
Sierra Leone Narrow Gauge D 28 9
Sirhowy Valley Line E 12 3
Sittingbourne to Ramsgate A 90 1
Slough to Newbury C 56 7
South African Two-foot gauge E 51 2
Southampton to Bournemouth A 42 0
Southend & Southminster BLs E 76 5
Southern Alpine Narrow Gauge F 22 2
Southern France Narrow Gauge C 47 5
South London Line B 46 6
South Lynn to Norwich City F 03 1
Southwold - Branch Line to A 15 4
Spalding - Branch Lines around E 52 9
Stafford to Chester F 34 5